Renaissance Dawning

South Africa – into the 21st century

Renaissance Dawning

South Africa – into the 21st century

Mike Freedman

ZEBRA

ZEBRA

First published by Zebra Press, an imprint of Southern Books
(a division of the New Holland Struik Publishing Group (Pty) Ltd.)
PO Box 5563, Rivonia, 2128, South Africa
Tel: (011) 807-2292
Fax: (011) 807-0506

First edition 1999

© in published work, Southern Books, 1999
© in text, Mike Freedman, 1999

All rights reserved. No part of this publication may be reproduced, stored in a retrieval system or transmitted, in any form or by any means, electronic, mechanical, photocopying, recording or otherwise, without the prior written permission of the copyright holder(s).

ISBN 1 86872 252 X

Cover design: Lindy Truswell
Typesetting and design: PG&A, Gauteng

Set in 12 on 14 pt Joanna

Reproduction by PG&A, Gauteng
Printed and bound by Creda Communications, Eliot Avenue, Epping II 7460

This book is dedicated to my children, Jade and Daniel, and all the children of this land.

introduction
to the first edition

In May 1994, the most famous political prisoner of our time became the president of our country. One hundred days later, newspapers and magazines analysed what had been done to make South Africa a better country for all its citizens. In May 1995, the report cards were marked again.

While speed is needed, politically and morally, too much haste usually provokes more confusion than accomplishment. Successful countries, like successful corporations, take time to evolve. Usually, at least 10 years are needed to make a significant difference. The first five years are spent thinking, planning and executing; the next five are spent building on the foundations, turning a success into a legend. It is hard to judge a company, or a country, on one year's results. It is harder still when there are no benchmarks.

In *Competing for the Future*, Gary Hamel and CK Prahalad write of the need for 'industry foresight'. The process starts with what could be, then works out the steps that have to be taken.

Throughout this book there are 'news cuttings' about South Africa from the year 2004 – 10 years after this country's first free and generally fair elections. These scenes from the future are mostly positive. Negative scenarios abound and cannot be ignored. Yet focusing on a positive future gives us the best chance of achieving one. The quest for blue skies starts with the belief they can be found.

In *The Lost Trails of the Transvaal*, TV Bulpin writes of how trails were formed by the migrating herds of wild animals; hunters followed, then the traders and trekkers. Some of these trails are now lost in the bush; others have become national highways. Similarly, the trails to the future already exist. You come across them in newspapers and magazines, although rarely on the front page or in leader articles. There are patterns and convergences in the minds of people who seem to have little in common.

I have talked to captains of industry and the unemployed, to citizens of a retirement village and children in a farm school. In over 100 individual interviews and group discussions, I discovered common threads. *Business Day* and *Sowetan* have given me different daily perspectives; *Financial Mail*, *Mail & Guardian*, *New Nation* and *Newsweek* have been part of my weekly intake; Compuserve and the Internet have enabled me to search the world.

In my quest I have met many people who generously gave me their time and shared their knowledge. To thank them individually would swell this book by many pages, and so I take this opportunity to thank them, collectively. (Specific acknowledgements and references appear at the end of the book.) I am especially grateful to my business clients who have shown faith in the Blue Skies process, and to my friends who encouraged me. Thanks to Alan Stokes for his provocations, to Clem Sunter for believing in this book before I did, to my editors Marga Collings and Sandra Coelho for their faith, questions and insights. Everyone who contributed has made this book richer; but if you disagree with any opinion or disprove any fact, the fault must be laid at my door alone.

My greatest support has been my family. My mother always knew I would write this book. It is of great sadness to me that she is not alive to see it. My father has been a tireless researcher, tracking down obscure statistics, references and people. Often, while I was writing one paragraph, he was finding material for the next. My children give me the motivation for my quest. And my wife, Prue, has been my sternest critic as well as my best pal. You have shown me the blue sky, when I only saw the storm. Thank you.

Mike Freedman
JOHANNESBURG
OCTOBER 1995

introduction
to the second edition

Since I wrote the first edition of this book, *Quest for Blue Skies*, the mood of South Africa has slipped from the euphoria of our miracle 1994 elections to the sobering realities of violent crime, corruption and the general feeling that political freedom has delivered far less than promised. Many despair, while others await another miracle. And some believe the future is ours to grab hold of and create.

This book is for the creators, the activists who will change this land. The people who can make the second miracle happen. Each chapter is a selection of possibilities. I invite you to read them in any order you wish. Agree, disagree, simply react. South Africa will become a world of storms or a renaissance dawning. The choice is ours.

Mike Freedman
Noordhoek, Western Cape
April 1999

contents

1. **THE ARCH OF DEMOCRACY**
   In the first decade of the 21st century, will South Africa be facing anarchy and chaos; or enjoying the first fruits of an economic renaissance? 1

2. **WELCOME TO THE USSA**
   The United States of Southern Africa can win respect and friends. Amongst them will be the multinational corporations that shape world affairs. 11

3. **THE OCEAN THAT JOINS US**
   Could the greatest trade opportunities for South Africa await in India, the country that soon will have the biggest middle class in the world? 20

4. **THREE-WHEELING THROUGH AFRICA**
   Three-wheelers can be mobile shops, meals on wheels, taxis and low-cost bakkies. They will enable tens of thousands of aspirant entrepreneurs to start their own businesses. 29

5. **CAN YOU MAKE MONEY OUT OF THE POOR?**
   Credit enables the poor to overcome their poverty. If the sophisticated South African banking system is going to deliver, it must offer more than money. 36

6. WHAT CAN YOU DO WITH DIRT?
How can townships thrive? Before you build a mall, or homes people can't afford, start a market.   44

7. BETTER THAN MONEY
Bartering is a growing trading mechanism. Nations, businesses, communities and the self-employed do it. Could bartering now lift Africa out of debt?   52

8. BACK TO THE LAND
The re-ruralisation of Africa. De-stress the cities with South African versions of Israeli kibbutzim and thriving new age small towns.   57

9. DE-ENGINEERING: THE CURE FOR SANDTONITIS
Many products and services are over-engineered. It is a marketing disease called 'Sandtonitis'. Happily, there is now a cure.   64

10. THE BIGGER PICTURE
While South Africa refinds her national pride, the world has gone global and Africa is an afterthought at best. How can we make a global impact?   75

11. NEVER RUB BOTTOMS WITH A PORCUPINE
We are not making the most of our natural resources. How can South Africa add significant value to her gold, trees and people?   86

12. HOOKED ON HEMP
Dagga puts food on the tables of 250 000 subsistence farmers and their families. Can the crop be harvested and used in morally acceptable ways?   99

13. RETURN OF THE WRIGGLIES
Mopane worms embrace their destiny; together with the world's insects they can fight global hunger.   107

contents

14. **ADVENTURES IN CYBERSPACE**
    The Internet will come of age when it gives the poor
    equal rights and opportunity. In the meantime,
    it is a wonderful medium with which South African
    entrepreneurs can go global.   115

15. *SIYABONGA*
    Tourism is becoming the world's largest industry. In
    South Africa it lies a poor fourth. We need a
    comprehensive strategy and a different attitude.   128

16. **THE JOBURG JOL**
    Gauteng will be the engine of southern Africa, and
    Johannesburg will be the heart of it. But how can Joburg
    be a great place to visit and a city its people enjoy?   140

17. **IT'S BETTER THAN BOURNEMOUTH**
    Is the world about to discover the retirement coast, from
    the Cape to Mozambique?   154

18. **THE TIME-SHARE BOERESTAAT**
    Will the beloved volkstaat ever amount to more than
    timeshare on a gamefarm?   160

19. **FLOWERS OF THE EAST**
    Can we turn the 25 million tons of fly ash we produce
    each year into golf courses, chrysanthemums,
    oysters and homes?   164

20. **THE THIRD WORLD WAR**
    South Africa is losing the battle against AIDS; over
    three million people are HIV positive. And everyone is affected.
    Can we turn the tide?   172

21. *EDUCERE:* **TO DRAW OUT**
    Needed: a new education system. Objective: prepare
    children for the job market of the future.   183

22. THE WOMEN OF AFRICA
For the women of Africa to be emancipated, they must first emancipate their men and reduce the levels of violence. 195

23. THE SQUATTER CAMP IN THE BOARDROOM
The people of South Africa need a shared vision and set of values if we want a true African renaissance. But we hardly know each other. 207

one

the arch of democracy

Freedom Day, South Africa: 27 April 2004

The dawn of what promises to be a clear, bright autumn day reflects across the gold and blue glass Arch of Democracy that straddles Johannesburg's Rissik Street. It is a monument to the new South Africa and houses the Gauteng International Trade Centre, shopping mall and hotel.

At midday, massed choirs will lead the Freedom Day parade from the Arch of Democracy, their multicoloured robes slowly forming the national flag. Following the singers along Rissik Street will be groups of children riding on floats, representing 27 schools that triumphed during 2003 in life-skills, sports, and creativity.

The next floats will include the southern African paratroopers, national sports teams, world boxing, athletic and golf champions, community leaders and traditional chiefs. Then, celebrating 10 years of progress, will be the floats of 27 companies ranging from a rural knitting co-operative to a multinational soft drink corporation. They are being given the honour of entering the Arch of Democracy as jets fly overhead, signwriting 'South Africa Salutes You', in what promises to be a wonderful day for a parade. Today is the 10th Anniversary of Freedom Day in South Africa, and the country is celebrating the beginnings of the African renaissance.

renaissance dawning

In 1994, South Africa languished near the bottom of the table in The World Competitiveness Report. The country was thirty-fifth out of 41; a losing nation. Now, just ten years later, South Africa is in the top 20.

After the company floats will come representatives of the poor and homeless on 27 sponsored living arts floats. When they reach the Amandla Statues, they will pause while the State President addresses them and, with the eyes of the world upon him, formally unveils the Statues. Made in Zimbabwe these figures, called the Amandla Statues, support a soaring pillar carved to represent the heroes and struggles of a continent. One face, of course, is known by all; and the pillar is being named after him. The southern hemisphere now has its very own new millennium Nelson's Column.

Behind the poor, the politicians will end the parade. Looking along Rissik Street, they will see thousands before them, representative of the millions they are empowered to lead, and in the minds of many will be the thoughts of Nelson Mandela, who likened a leader to a shepherd: *He walks behind the flock, allowing the most nimble to go on ahead while the rest follow, making sure those at the side do not wander off, and those at the back do not fall behind.*

World Internet News

Currently, South Africa Incorporated is not in great shape. Struggling near the bottom of the world competitiveness league, we suffer from mistrust, arrogance, racism, violence, male chauvinism, protectionist policies, unhealthy cartels, short-term thinking and a lack of training. There is a chasm between the squatter camp and the boardroom.

Doomsday scenarios abound: the economy is a mess, the rand is monopoly money, it is impossible to achieve the growth needed to significantly lower unemployment levels. The cancer of violence resists treatment, and when the expectations of the young are not met, as poverty and homelessness radicalise more and more in the townships, as the one-time favoured minority are passed over and eased out, as AIDS lays waste to millions of lives, so growing anarchy and chaos will plunge South Africa into a twenty-first-century nightmare of decaying cities, mindless killing and retribution while a terrified middle class flees, taking Krugerrands and diamonds, leaving over-bonded homes, pools and cars to the baying mob ...

Armageddon can begin here. This country has the weaponry, the ethnic divisions, the anger and a history of deep injustice that can spill over to ignite greater hatred and atrocities than seen in Bosnia and Rwanda. If South Africa Inc. does not create wealth, its future is bleak.

Every South African has a choice – to make our land a killing ground, or one of the few good places left on earth to raise a family and make one's mark. In the dawn of the new millennium, South Africa Inc. must begin to prosper or it will start to die.

the cultures of entitlement and intolerance

An unjust society created a culture of entitlement. Protest took the form of non-payment, non-compliance, and eventual violence. Repressive poverty justified crime. The first free elections raised expectations and dissatisfied voters now ask: 'Where is my house, Mr President? Where is my car?' The lost generation who sacrificed their education for the struggle expect a payback. They want to know: 'What was it all for, Mr President? Where is my job? Why are the whites still rich and we still poor?' For decades the outlaw mentality was encouraged, and now that it is ingrained, the rules have suddenly changed.

In Hammanskraal, 200 hawkers created a market near a bus station. Developers bought the site for a shopping mall and offered to relocate the hawkers. 'If you try to move us, we will burn down your place. We have a right to be here,' they replied. People never employed by a company picket its factory; they have a right to jobs. The head office of a national retailer is surrounded by strikers bearing signs that demand 'Merit increases for all!' A multiple taxi-owner has never paid taxes; what started as a refusal to support an unjust regime has become money in his pocket. A regular corporate tax-payer folds his arms and says: 'I pay 50 cents in the rand; I pay 14 per cent VAT. I fund the government. What is the ANC doing for me?' Everyone feels entitled. Strikes multiply, company assets find their way into overseas bank accounts and the silent majority still wait, like the cargo cult of New Guinea, for gifts to rain from the sky.

The culture of intolerance lives in the underbelly of entitlement. Students, husbands, taxi-owners and cowherders settle their differences with knives, guns, burning tyres and pangas. Belonging to the 'wrong' political party is often a death sentence. Two motorists park their cars on the motorway verge and blow each other away in an urban high noon.

This culture of intolerance is provoked by agents of disruption on the radical left and reactionary right who believe they must burn down before they build. It is intensified by an uneven crime to punishment ratio, and the flood of illegal weaponry and drugs that swamp sub-Saharan Africa. Our murder rate is 10 times higher than that of the United States, and every violent death is a breeding ground for revenge. The fences rise, the dogs grow fiercer and civilisation is lost.

leadership and fellowship

> *'A true leader must have a vision of reconciliation.'* NELSON MANDELA

> *'Leadership is a matter of intelligence, trustworthiness, humaneness, courage and sternness.'* SUN TZU, The Art of War

The cultures of entitlement and intolerance were born in a moral vacuum. They flourish in the confusion and conflict of change. They feed off poverty, disease and a sense of hopelessness. If there is no sense of national vision, no shared values, what is there to prevent the deadly brew from poisoning us all?

We need political, community and business leaders to create and communicate brave, powerful visions; we also need rich and poor, black and white, young and old to adopt a common set of values. While visions may change – every American president except perhaps George Bush had one – values are constant: 'life, liberty and the pursuit of happiness' is not negotiable.

Of course, leaders must do far more than debate vision and values. History will judge them on what they deliver. We have political leaders who are new at the job. They range from inspired to inept, some possessing cast-iron integrity and some who are hopelessly corrupt. We have community leaders who were trained to destroy and now must build; many of the best are being promoted to regional and national positions, leaving a scramble for power at local levels too often won by the most venal and violent. And we have business leaders who are slow to relinquish old ways. Amongst all the dramatic changes, little has happened in South African boardrooms. In parliament there are 80 per cent new faces; in the boardrooms, most of the old guard still rule. Many business leaders have turned from anxious liberals into worried conservatives. Some are like the prizefighter with one too many fights under his belt. Good in his day, he is now punch-drunk and scared. Other visionary business leaders, still to reach their prime, are taking on global challenges as South Africa shifts from their centre of consciousness.

We need to find and train the leaders that will make southern Africa internationally competitive; leaders that can see and take their followers beyond narrow interests to the good of all.

There is a tradition in this land of ubuntu. It means: 'I become a person only through other people. How my community sees me determines in my eyes the person that I am'. Ubuntu is doing something for a person in need without expecting anything in return. It is based on fellowship and collaboration. How ubuntu began is lost in myth. Perhaps it was a response to this harsh and generous land; rain, and the lack of it, may have seeded ubuntu. In times of plenty, everyone has enough to share and enjoy. In times of scarcity, sharing is survival. Ubuntu is like a plant rooted in the arid African soil. It can lie dormant and undetected for long periods. Then, when the rains finally come, ubuntu begins to flower once more.

> *'As soon as we are accorded the dignity of being treated like people, we behave in our natural way. We have an ethic that is called ubuntu, which describes what the Europeans call civilised behaviour. It is not alien to us. It is part of our language, our rituals and our ceremonies.'* AGGREY KLAASTE, editor of The Sowetan, April 1994

In a Mpumalanga township, half a dozen people sit around a table talking about ubuntu. They say it is dead, a victim of the torn social fabric. 'My aunt allowed a stranger to stay with her and he stole her things. It happened twice. Now she turns people away. She is unhappy because she has broken the custom, but what can she do? We don't trust one another,' says Jeff D.

As he speaks, one of the men in the group helps himself to a cigarette from the pack lying on the table; the others follow suit. No one asks permission; no one is put out. You cannot tell to whom the pack belongs; the sharing is natural. When I remark on it, saying I have just seen a small sign of ubuntu, Jeff replies: 'You only kiss those people you favour; you don't kiss people you don't know.'

Ubuntu has been battered, yet it still lives. It is the opposite of the Western self-centred universe. And it could be the next multinational way of doing business because, worldwide, corporations are searching for their souls.

ubuntu and the caring corporation

Being able to read a balance sheet used to be the best entry ticket into a multinational boardroom. Now times they are 'a-changing'. Soft issues, such as employee happiness and customer loyalty, are recognised as major bottom-line contributors and the sincerity of companies is a global topic. Aware consumers ask: 'What kind of company makes these products? What do you give back to society?'

Consumer boycotts hurt bottom lines and cost millions in corrective public relations. Boycotts against Shell to protest the company dumping an oil rig into the sea caused lost sales of R100 million a day in Germany and England. Some consumers who reacted out of moral conviction have found service they prefer somewhere else; service Shell took a lifetime to cultivate and one ill-considered decision to lose.

Companies that care for, attract and keep the best people enjoy good supplier relations, turn customers into converts and gain the approval of society. They listen more attentively, see unmet needs more clearly and possess the will to change themselves before trying to change the world. Perhaps the next giant oil rigs will be designed for disassembly, and Shell will sponsor research into creating artificial rig reefs that support marine life.

A company is our new community. We know more people at work than in our neighbourhood. Moral values are strengthened or weakened from eight to five. If there is no social concern shown at work, there will be far less shown in society.

'Happiness of man is built on mental stability and material affluence. To serve the foundation of happiness through making man's life affluent is the duty of the manufacturer.

Profit comes in compensation for contribution to society. Profit is a yardstick with which to measure the degree of social contribution made by an enterprise.

If the enterprise tries to earn a reasonable profit but fails to do so, the reason is that the degree of its social contribution is still insufficient.' KONOSUKE MATSUSHITA, founder of Matsushita, the world's largest producer of electronic products

The cultures of entitlement and intolerance can be transformed by the nurturing of the culture of ubuntu in caring corporations. Profit is not 'look at how well I've done', but rather, the recognition society gives due to the service rendered. As multinationals search for meaning, South Africans discover it in their own backyards.

Ubuntu does not reach down to accept compromise; it reaches up to find consensus. The greater challenge is not to fight a war but to find common ground. Often, ubuntu looks like all indaba and no action – months and even years filled with long meetings where the ground continually shifts, things previously agreed on are suddenly questioned, and finally, when it's time for signatures, the chosen representatives are declared non-representative.

An international report on South African non-competitiveness reflects on problems caused by the 'time-consuming consultation process versus active decision making'. But decisions that are not trusted will not endure. And there are few reasons, given our history, for workers to believe in management. If you did not trust your boss before May 1994, why should you do so now?

Ubuntu may be long-winded, and the slow, searching process can lose its way, but what is the alternative? Adversarial unions and management can fulfil their own worst predictions. The new nation is too easily redivided along class and colour lines. But internal fights are not the way to gain world business; you don't win the race by shooting yourself in the foot.

Ubuntu is satisfactory in theory, but how can the managing director preach it all day to his workers then go home in his Mercedes, splashing them in the rain while they wait for a bus? When a machine operator wants to loan R2 000 to pay for a relative's funeral, does the financial director tell him it is not company policy, then fly off with his wife to the company game-lodge? The workers cannot share the boss's office, salary, stock options, overseas trips or cigars. They cannot down tools and have a 10-hour indaba every time a decision has to be made that affects them. If they are employed by a large corporation, their chief executive might just as well be on another planet.

Ubuntu works when there is trust, common purpose and tradition. Those conditions exist in a rural African community. But there is little trust between workers and management; there is no common purpose. While the tradition of ubuntu is questioned by urban blacks, it remains a vague concept for most whites. Ubuntu is becoming a management mantra, but before it can be a reality, some basic values need to be reassessed.

If the company purpose is to make money for shareholders and workers have no stake in this, ubuntu has no foundation. In the culture of ubuntu, a king is a king by virtue of his subjects; in most Eurocentric companies, the managers are chosen and assessed by the few above not the many below. The ubuntu leader listens to all who want to speak and then searches for a consensus of views; companies usually operate in secrecy. Because of their nature, unions and management are in constant conflict: while unions demand more jobs and more pay, management insist on retrenchments and minimum wage-hikes.

Every company in this country needs a period of self-examination and its own truth and reconciliation commission to clear the anger, misunderstandings and guilt of the past. Consensus can then be reached about shared values and a common future.

re-engineering the country

'The enemy of reconstruction and development is unemployment. If unemployment continues to grow, a programme to address poverty will be like trying to catch water in a sieve.' JAY NAIDOO

South Africa needs more jobs. This means local corporations must become more productive to compete and win in the global marketplace. America has shown how re-engineering can cut costs and speed up processes. Jobs are shed and management layers are flattened. This presents South African companies with the paradox of increasing employment by reducing employment. How can a local union accept half a loaf today for jam tomorrow? And if you lose your job for the common good, will you feel spiritually uplifted?

If companies alone are re-engineered, the process will fail. South Africa needs re-engineering, and it starts from the ground up, rather than being imposed from the top down. Layers of bureaucracy must be eliminated to make government faster, better and less expensive. Corruption must be weeded out. The mass of law-abiding citizens must be protected and given equal opportunities. The economic climate must become entrepreneur friendly, encouraging the wealth-makers and employers of tomorrow to flourish. While banning smoking in public places and demanding an affirmative action national cricket team are worthy of debate, government must focus on the fundamentals.

Corruption, violence, high taxes and artificial restraints on free trade all retard increased levels of employment. So does mistrust between business and trade unions. Each obstacle has to be removed before South Africa can begin to grow. And while we have many natural resources from sunshine to gold, focused education, training and support are all necessary for this country to realise its full potential.

turning ubuntu into homes

Fifty-five thousand people living in squatter camps around the country have joined in groups, usually of 60 to 150 members, to save money for a most unlikely dream – their own homes. Of those, 85 per cent are women. They are domestic workers, pensioners, casual labourers and hawkers. They make clothes, grow vegetables, dig pit latrines, collect firewood and water. Their average household income is less than R700 a month and they save as little as five cents a day, every day. They belong to the South African Homeless People's Federation who say:

'Our main aim is not to collect money; we're collecting people.'

From the Piesang River to Mossel Bay, homes are being built. Within their families, women find builders, carpenters and plumbers. They negotiate in the leather-chaired boardrooms, the township backyards and the halls of bureaucracy dealing with men who have never encountered a group of women in the construction business, especially women who are poor and black. Homeless women become project managers, planners, accountants, pipe-layers and builders, while they still try to save. Bureaucracy and other agendas slow them down and frustrate their intentions, yet they find strength in each other and the federation grows daily. Over 2 500 houses have been completed. The women of Africa see a life beyond the rows of dusty shacks.

On the other side of the equation, world-class banks and construction companies are gearing up to build for the not-so-poor. The women's co-operatives may not build as many houses, but they will show how they want their homes to look and how far they can spread their limited budgets. They will provoke new low-cost ways to build and finance homes. They show that having no place to live and no job can be overcome by hope, mutual help and the will to make something happen. They are the grass-roots of reconstruction and development.

The cultures of entitlement and intolerance, if left to spread, will choke these roots. A national vision and shared values will protect them and encourage growth. Most of all, each of us has a duty to make a positive contribution. It is not a question of what the country can do for us, but rather, under the Arch of Democracy, what can we do for ourselves, each other and southern Africa.

two
welcome to the USSA

The missionaries of enlightened capitalism

It is 10 days before Christmas in Beira, Mozambique, and 23-year-old Kate Sadowski sounds frazzled.

'I've got a broken-down truck 50 kilometres outside Xai-Xai. It's 30 degrees in the shade and five tons of prawns are slowly defrosting.' Her nose delicately quivers at the thought.

'Our chief mechanic is at his brother's wedding, his assistant has tick-bite fever and our emergency back-up has gone fishing. This isn't logistics; it's a nightmare. Unless Piri-Piri Truckers has someone I can use.'

'Aren't they the opposition?' I ask.

'Sure,' she smiles at my confusion. 'Welcome to the USSA; that's the way things work here.'

A week earlier I was in the Zambian Copper Belt. Bud Graham, a 25-year-old star quarterback, newly qualified in international law, was assisting the biggest mining trade union. They were in an urgent caucus, considering strike action over some proposed ablution blocks.

The construction company that won the contract followed specifications set out by the mining company. The unions then said they had not been consulted. The meeting had to expand to include a host of grievances.

'If we had a fan here,' Bud said, sweat pouring down his face, 'you know what would have just hit it.'

Kate and Bud are amongst the young missionaries of enlightened capitalism who spread the dogma of free enterprise through the United States of Southern Africa. They are on secondment from multinational companies who combine world upliftment programmes with two years of TIM (Total Immersion Management).

Global strategists debate the competitive merits of the United States, Asia and Europe. They opine on the Euro, ponder the buying power of two billion consumers in China and India, then speculate on the potential of Russia and South America.

Africa is an afterthought. Soft drink and cigarette companies see growth in the oldest continent, while other multinationals feel they must have a presence here. On the ground, the battles for brand share look fierce, but from the global perspective, they are minor skirmishes. No wars are won or lost here.

A national importer of hi-tech equipment complained that his orders weren't being filled fast enough. He was politely told that there were temporary shortages, and as South Africa's requirements were less than those of a single store in Chicago he could kindly wait in line.

Others see Africa as a basket-case. Although the new South Africa is a possible exception, a country is like a house or store: however much you change the interior, your position determines your value.

Most African countries are being buried under mountains of debt. They lack infrastructure, vision and hope. The colonial hangover retarded a spread of industry, keeping the continent a slave to world commodity prices, tribalism and the weather. While over 750 million people live in Africa, only 0,4% of world export of manufactured goods come from African countries. The gross domestic product (GDP) of South Africa is less than the sales of Exxon; and the GDPs of eight African nations are less than the sales of any one of the top 500 USA corporations. Are we at the wrong end of a global megatrend?

charity and trade begin at home

South Africa has too much on its plate to become deeply involved in the turbulence of Africa. And yet we cannot cut ourselves away from her, we cannot pretend she doesn't exist and we cannot hide behind electrified walls.

Many South Africans spent years as exiles in neighbouring states. Now these neighbours would like to share our relative prosperity. Protecting yourself against and shooting your former hosts is ungrateful in the extreme. Besides, we need some competitive local trading partners.

As Africa trades more with itself, it will grow stronger, creating regional competencies and world-class strengths. Yet trading in war zones and areas of famine and corruption are not assignments to give your brightest and best. Not yet, anyhow.

South Africa must spread the peace dividend beyond her borders. The people of this subcontinent are tired of endless fighting. Yet wars don't stop at the wave of a wand and dictators are not in the habit, unless nudged, of removing themselves.

are we africans or south africans?

Many white South Africans still shudder to think of themselves as African. They look to Europe and America for role models, and while there is a huge amount to be learnt from overseas, there is much that Africa can teach us as well. If we do not come to terms with our African identity, what unique thing can we offer the rest of the world?

Until recently, 'Made in South Africa' was a pariah label; now it is quite acceptable. Yet 'Made in Africa' on tractors or clothes is unlikely to command a premium. Local and multinational companies aim to produce world-class quality products in Africa; few aspire to African quality. Isn't it a bit like Irish logic or English cooking? Being written off by the world is no joke.

If we South Africans continue to deny this continent, we will lose our roots. To embrace our Africanness is to embark on a journey of shared learning. Where the journey will take us is unclear, but that has never stopped the great adventurers of the past. A unified South Africa is not a goal, but a milestone.

the african common market

The Indian Ocean Rim is already drawing the Eastern Seaboard together. Trade between South Africa, Mozambique, Tanzania and Kenya is growing fast. The people of Mozambique are beginning to reap the peace harvest. Their imports include capital equipment, hard evidence of growing optimism. Portuguese businessmen are back in Maputo, reliving old days at the Polana. The harbour is being rebuilt, the rail links upgraded and prawn aficionados have the choice of 30 restaurants, in place of two a few years ago.

As Gauteng becomes the industrial powerhouse of Africa, it will need to be fed and watered. Zimbabwe, Zambia, Uganda and Tanzania can all provide. Farmers from South Africa are looking at these horizons, and in the dawn of the next millennium a new trek to the south and east will begin.

Kenya, South Africa and Zimbabwe are the three most industrialised countries in southern Africa. Whilst South Africa is the core economy in the south, Kenya is the core of East Africa and Zimbabwe is the key to the food-basket. A three-sided trade and military agreement, if the parties can share the vision, is easier and far quicker to put together than a 12-sided one. Between them, the big three will have a patchwork of trade agreements with each nation in southern and eastern Africa. They will give birth to the USSA – the United States of Southern Africa.

The political voice of the alliance must persuade the world to reschedule overpowering debt repayments of countries such as Angola. The military power of the USSA must be respected throughout the region; tough love can make the economic union work.

the mozambican option

On a map it looks logical: split up Mozambique; it was only a colonial invention anyway. The south, with the prize of Maputo, goes to South

welcome to the ussa

Africa, giving Gauteng a port that's closer than Durban. The centre, with the prize of Beira, gives land-locked Zimbabwe a dreamed-of coastline. Then the north can be divided between Zambia, Malawi and Tanzania.

If you consider ethnic groups and languages, it is a natural division. The country is desperately poor and can hardly be called unified. The split helps everyone except those in power and that is one reason why it will never happen. The other is that the rest of Africa, also carved up by the colonial powers, prefers the imperfect *status quo* to the chaos of movable borders.

While Mozambique looks destined to remain in one piece, its leaders can open up the trade routes, giving South Africa, Zimbabwe, Zambia and Malawi free access to the sea. The Maputo Corridor is the start of the process. In return, the poorest country in the world can become the twenty-first-century nerve centre of Indian Ocean trade.

afro-cops

Before any serious investment happens in countries such as Angola, there must be sustainable peace. The world was moved by the transition of power in South Africa, but that well of goodwill is fast running dry. It is time to exert our moral authority. If we do not help each other now, we will be left alone to sort out our problems.

Peace treaties are insufficient. Credible back-up will ensure that the treaties are kept. The existence and threat of the South African Defence Force stopped many from taking the warriors' path. The subcontinent will be safer for people and trade once a Southern African Peace-keeping Force is in place.

It can no longer be someone else's problem. The United Nations suffered from tragic inaction in Bosnia and throughout the former USSR. The United States stumbled in Africa, then announced they were not going to be world cops any longer.

The Southern African Peace-keeping Force, funded by grateful countries who no longer have to do the dirty work, will absorb many rebel and government troops. The force will wage war on hunger and disease. It will monitor elections, calm passions, build bridges and help communities. When necessary, it will fight for peace.

The battle-weary factions of southern Africa have no global paymasters, no great cause and little moral stature. An indigenous peace-keeping force, rolling out democracy from the high ground of the new South Africa, is the best chance everyone has of a disaster-free future. Yet peace cannot co-exist with poverty. Hope must replace desperation.

intermediate technologies

Our first priorities are not six-lane highways and shopping malls. People need roads to interconnect their villages. They want to rebuild the trading stores.

They are tired of carrying water up rocky paths. Rolling along a fat plastic drum with a string through the middle is far more effective than an empty promise of a pipeline. While villagers wait for electricity, a stove that works on solar power or transfers heat more efficiently saves time and trees. Clockwork radios and torches replace batteries with armpower.

Agriculture in township backyards and plots are a means of survival. The mealies and beans supplement a meagre diet. Flowers growing in a shack settlement are sold on street-corners in town. When Africa is allowed to work, it is resourceful. Instead of food parcels that reach the wrong hands, we need chemists to experiment with fertiliser using ingredients that urban mini-farmers can easily source.

Intermediate technologies enable the poor to do what they do more efficiently. It is one step up the ladder, not a leap. It does not impose Western solutions. And it's affordable. That means something can happen now, while all the grander plans are debated and reshaped.

the prosperity corps

As governments come together to create the peace-keepers, so business can unite to provide the prosperity-makers. Upliftment needs trained people and capital. America created the Peace Corps; now South Africa has the opportunity to begin the 'Prosperity Corps'. It will be an army of young accountants, agricultural engineers, entrepreneurs, geologists, lawyers and project managers who spend two to three years in a southern African state and are committed to their host's blend of African socialism, democracy and free enterprise.

They will help to restore the coffee plantations in Angola; discover reserves of natural gas in Mozambique; develop agriculture, trade and people throughout the region. Fresh from MBA courses, these young missionaries will live amongst communities on the cusp of hunger and hope. They will transfer skills, making a real difference to many thousands of lives. And they will learn how to care.

The Prosperity Corps can start in South Africa and spread around the world. 'Total Immersion Management' (TIM) can become the global way to put a multinational company's brightest and best on a fast-track of learning and contributing. Major corporations would sponsor their rising stars to work for companies and organisations in developing countries. Their mission will be to share knowledge. While it may be costly, it will not be charity. TIM is an investment in the whole person, as well as a country. It will polish a company image, and when the young missionaries return, they will bring back an understanding that research just can't obtain.

Foreign aid was once the prerogative of governments. Now it is becoming corporate investment policy, and multinationals are far better networked than any government. Ambassadors live in embassies. Traders spend their lives in the market-place. For instance, if you want to know whether an area is winning or losing and you don't want to wait for trade figures that are debatable and out of date, talk to the chewing-gum manufacturer. When people have less cash in their pockets, they stop chewing. When the change rattles again, they chew.

The Prosperity Corps will be the eyes and ears of aware companies, teaching as well as learning. They are not corporate colonialists, robbing locals of jobs. They will be advisers and facilitators, offering their youth, energy and education. Spreading out from South Africa they will discover the less travelled paths that one day will become our commercial highways.

the power of africa

The USSA has the power to fight illiteracy, poverty and disease. It will attract international investment and aid. The twenty-first century could have its first great legend; its own prodigal family.

renaissance dawning

Heroic projects will tie us together. Hydroelectric power from the Congo River in Zaire can provide southern Africa with 50 to 100 times more electric power than the Cahora Bassa scheme, while conserving coal and the environment. Exploration, unhindered by war and corruption, will unlock the secret treasures of our mineral-rich continent. Instead of importing oil from overseas, a pipeline will link the Angolan oilfields with Sasol. The parched Highveld could draw water from Kariba.

Unhampered by industry of the past, southern Africa will be a testing ground for technologies of the future. Eskom, with no additional capital expenditure, can charge six million electric cars overnight. South Africa's vehicle population is five million. Eskom is building prototype electric bakkies and taxis. If they are successful, mass production could happen in a neighbouring state that has no motor manufacturing industry.

The USSA will not happen quickly or easily, and there will be many pitfalls along the way. The continent's poverty, disease, crime and wars will threaten to overwhelm our own fragile recovery. Then why should we get involved with our rag-tag neighbours? Because you can have a beautiful home, but if it is in an unsafe area, guard-dogs and fences will not be enough to protect you inside it.

For South Africa, the choice is clear: embrace Africa or be swamped by Africa.

'The union meeting went on through two hot days and nights,' Bud Graham wrote to me. 'Finally, the vote was for a strike.

'I know it's right and it's wrong ... and I'm learning that law school was too clear-cut. The workers weren't consulted and that is dehumanising. Yet they were going to have something far better than they had before. What will this strike achieve, apart from hardship? The mine-owners say they cannot afford more production loss, and the new ablution facilities may never be built. I could fight that in the courts, but who wins?'

In her small Beira office, Kate Sadowski is celebrating. The second mechanic of Piri-Piri Truckers was flown to Xai-Xai in a small plane. He then fixed the truck and its refrigeration unit in time for Gauteng to enjoy prawns at Christmas.

'The Beira Prawn and Lobster Company is giving everyone a January bonus,' she says. 'If those prawns had rotted, people would have been out of jobs.'

Her Mozambican boss reflects on the influence of these missionaries. 'We highly value Kate's skills and contributions,' he says, 'but that doesn't mean we will all eat Big Macs, salute the stars and stripes and become born-again capitalists.

'African socialism has been around since the dawn of man. We believe helping others is helping yourself, and that is what Kate is doing. As she influences and develops us, we hope we influence and develop her. When she goes home, she will carry a little of Africa in her heart and mind.'

three
the ocean that joins us

Rubicon 2000 crosses to Bombay

As grateful as we all are for our special relationship with India, I feel a voice must be raised to protest the imbalance.

Last week I enquired about a Rubicon 2000 and was astounded to hear that every unsold bottle was on the water to Bombay. And most Indians never even drink wine; it is not part of their tradition or culture.

However, in the last 10 years, globalism has invaded the Indian sub-continent, and fine wines are now the fashionable thing to drink. Due to our special relationship, most of the wine is coming from this country. The Australians could have done their bit if they knew how to make quality wine, but most of them still think a cabernet is a place for files.

I consulted an auditor friend, who observed that if only one Indian in a thousand drinks a single bottle of quality South African wine a month, our entire annual output would be swallowed up.

While this may seem an extreme situation, it does raise an important question. As the twenty-first century progresses, will the lion of Africa become too dependent on the new tiger of Asia?

Letter to the editor, Natal Times, January 2004

the ocean that joins us

A billion people live in India, 35% of them under the age of 15. During the first decades of the twenty-first century, it will become the most populous nation on earth, overtaking China.

Between 200 million and 300 million people in India are economically active. They live in mega-cities such Bombay, Calcutta, and Delhi. (These three cities alone will soon house more people than the whole of South Africa.) They choose what toothpaste to use, what food to eat, what clothes and jewellery to buy. Only the United States has a larger middle-class population.

Ninety million people in India are actual and potential share investors. The country has 22 stock exchanges.

The largest watch company in the world is not Rolex, Omega, Swatch or Seiko. It is not from Switzerland or Japan. It is Titan, from India. Clothing manufacturers in Cape Town and Durban drown under the flood of low-cost imports from India and China. And as we enter the information age, India is emerging as the lowest-cost producer of top quality computer programs. This creates a global knowledge centre. In India, unless you are content to be a subsistence farmer, you need a BSc to find a job – although a Masters degree is preferable.

In the last decade the Indian economy averaged over five per cent real growth each year, and the country's annual inflation rate has been eight per cent.

After China, India is the world's largest gold consumer, using almost 500 tons a year. The whole of Europe uses less than 350 tons. Gold is part of Indian tradition and ritual; 60 million Indians buy that precious metal annually.

The huge, rapidly growing middle class has a spending power only recently unshackled by the expansion of the economy. This is the world's largest experiment in enlightened capitalism and the opportunities beckon every serious global corporation. The country has only 10 million telephones and 33 million televisions; it lacks ports, powerplants and roads.

However, half of the population is illiterate and most are trapped in poverty. Forty per cent of the population – almost 400 million people – cannot afford to eat properly. Natural disasters are now compounded by tensions between India, Pakistan and China. The nuclear poker game, when played by aggressive regionalists and firebrand socialists, has an unpredictable outcome. But for all its poverty, droughts, floods, religious, ethnic and political schisms, India remains more stable, democratic and pro free enterprise than China, Russia and much of Africa.

This vast market has suddenly appeared on business radar screens, like Atlantis re-emerging from the sea. American companies have been quick to enter this new-found land. Throughout Asia, American investment lags behind Japan, while in India, over 50 per cent of foreign proposals approved in the last few years bear the mark of the stars and stripes. It's the promised land of Chryslers and Coke, where America Inc. can grow even more powerful.

The English language is a natural link between the United States and India. It makes business easier and quicker. But South Africa and India are joined by more than our common tongue.

the oceans theory of history

Oceans do not divide. Through exploration, migration and trade, they join the countries whose shores they touch.

The past belonged to the Mediterranean, with Greece and Italy dominant in trade and culture.

The near-past was the Atlantic Age, with France, Great Britain and the east coast of America. This is the Age of the Pacific, featuring Japan, the Pacific Rim countries and the American west coast.

Does the future lie across the Indian Ocean? A billion people in India allied with the powerhouse of Africa makes a potent world statement. The Indian Ocean Rim is already being discussed by politicians and global strategists. A working group of seven countries (Australia, India, Kenya, Mauritius, Oman, Singapore and South Africa) met in Mauritius in March 1995 to set up the Indian Ocean Rim (IOR) as a forum for government, business and academia.

Various blueprints of the IOR exist. South Africa wants to include Pakistan, as well as most of southern Africa, while Australia would push for a military treaty to restrain India's navy.

Mauritius, which is promoting the IOR concept strongly, could become the Brussels of the union, a mid-way point where the group's politicians and civil servants can enjoy endless debates in the off-season. The IOR may be 10 to 15 years in the future, but we have begun our journey towards it.

Indonesia is the world's fourth most populous country, while the Gulf States are still amongst the richest. They will, by nature of their geography, gravitate to the alliance. Thirty countries border the Indian Ocean; only 20 per cent of their trade is currently between them. A meaningful economic grouping will cause a tectonic shift in global trade.

Some government strategists ponder an even bigger picture – an alliance of the South and East. South America, Africa and India – the weaker partners in world trade bonding in a geographic and psychographic union at the centre of which would be southern Africa. While these dreams slowly gain substance, the heart of the union already exists.

blood ties with south africa

Over one million Asians live in South Africa; the majority are under 30. Nearly all have families in India. They are our natural ambassadors. The town of Chatsworth has the biggest Indian population of any town outside India. It's beginning to bustle.

Traders first sailed the Indian Ocean 5 000 years ago in search of gold and slaves. Today we wear shirts made of Indian cotton, eat authentic curries and know an Indian shop that stays open after normal working hours. We may also, without knowing, take medicine and use computer software from India.

The people of India and South Africa have many shared values, including compassion, reconciliation, the extended family and communal help. The Western way of life touches us all materially. In return, the Western world begins to absorb the spiritual truths of the East and the South.

Mahatma Gandhi spent his formative years in South Africa. The lessons he learnt here returned with him to his home country, guiding his people through their most difficult times. His teachings, his humility and love have flowed back across the ocean during our own long, painful journey. Our first cricket tour to India after the apartheid years became a symbolic act of world acceptance.

non, je ne le parle pas

The English and the French live on opposite shores of a sea you can swim across, yet they have never befriended each other. Although only 22 miles apart (and that's part of the problem), they refuse to learn each other's language.

India and South Africa are eight hours flying time apart. By ship, a container takes 10 to 15 days from warehouse door to door, yet we are closer than most neighbours because of our colonial past. Other former European colonies spoke Portuguese, Spanish, Italian, French, German and Dutch. We were lucky.

Thanks to those other ex-colonials, the Americans, English is a basic necessity for global communications. CNN, MTV and Hollywood cover the world. Eighty-five per cent of the Internet is in English.

We need to talk to each other without interpreters. We cannot wait two days to translate e-mail. If *vous ne parlez pas* English, you miss out on world news, entertainment and trade. English is the language of global business. Children around the world are learning it. As long as the school rule is English plus one, 11 official languages are fine.

Indians and South Africans can already communicate company to company as well as community to community. We share the language of the new millennium.

more affordable housing

South Africa's housing costs are amongst the highest in the developing world. The subsidies and repayments needed for our proposed 1,5 million new homes will put the economy under enormous pressure. In India, the need for homes is much greater. Since 1970, an Indian government enterprise called Hudco has brought together technology and finance to give millions of the urban and rural poor an affordable roof over their heads.

Hudco has developed over five million homes, upgraded a million more and provided three million site and service units. Between 1992 and 1997 Hudco achieved as much as it did in its first 20 years. And the five-year plan started in 1997 projected more homes were built than in its total history.

Hudco has come to South Africa, displaying affordable housing technologies. It uses waste materials, such as fly ash, and natural materials like mud to make bricks. The organisation is involved in schemes ranging from low-cost sanitation to night shelters for pavement dwellers. It has training centres across India that encourage the jobless to 'earn while you learn'.

Hudco is not a charity; it operates on the principle of 'profitability with social justice'. If we adopt the same approach to affordable housing, more will be built for less. Alternative technologies would no longer be buried under conventional wisdoms, bureaucracies and cartels.

two-way trades

As South Africa opens its markets, textiles and clothes from India have poured into the country. Lower prices give more South Africans the chance to dress well and decorate their homes. Will local manufacturers suffer? If the market grows and they cannot survive, something is seriously wrong.

We have lived too long inside this cocoon of low productivity, slow delivery and poor service. We need strategies to thrive in the real world. And the first strategy for a product, a company or a country is: if you're not competitive, don't compete. Our unwieldy clothing factories close and in the midst of growing unemployment we can learn from our economic victors how women at home in their villages can be organised to create virtual factories. It is a 'back to the future' concept that works for India – and for Benetton in Italy.

Generic pharmaceuticals from India will halve the prices we pay. The cost of prescription drugs in South Africa is amongst the highest in the world. Throughout India, the poor can afford a doctor and medicine.

renaissance dawning

We also will pay less for quality computer software. American vendors and end-users rate Indian software amongst the world's best, yet a systems analyst in India receives one-seventh of the salary of his or her South African counterpart. Our banks can save millions, as can health and educational services.

Other imports include dyes (we make none of our own), natural rubber cross-ply tyres (for rough and rutted roads) and Darjeeling tea (for discerning taste buds).

What can we offer India? South African industry is mostly uncompetitive, but natural blessings come to our rescue. Rock phosphate, wool and steel may sound unglamorous, yet they can bring in over a billion rand a year. Minerals such as platinum and plutonium will be in growing demand, as will fruit and fruit juices.

Gold jewellery manufacture is a multi-billion-dollar business. Today, South Africa can learn production skills from India. Within a decade, when Asia consumes more gold than the rest of the world, we should be selling the finished product to that continent rather than the raw material.

Retailing in South Africa is a world-class operation. In India, the traditional momma and poppa shops still rule. Superstores, chains and malls are almost unknown. The megastore of New Delhi measures 3 000 square metres; elsewhere in India, 1 000 square metres is big. Joint ventures with South African retail groups can discover modern needs and transform a traditional industry. If we don't do it, we can be sure the Americans will.

At the moment, tourism between our countries mostly consists of South African Asians visiting their family homes. But as the 200 million middle-class Indian population grows, so the rupees can flow this way. Travel agencies will offer east-coast business safaris from Kenya to Cape Town, with some golf and young Ghandi pilgrimages as optional extras.

In South Africa as well as India we drive on the left side of the road and that takes us down interesting avenues. Used BMWs have been exported from South Africa to India. There they confer instant prestige; here second-hand prices are firmer, helping new car sales. As BMW South Africa begins to cut costs and focus on manufacturing the three-series, the vast Asian market welcomes them.

The ships would return full of three-wheelers, enabling new entrepreneurs to connect big business with township residents. As South Africa caters for the middle class, so India provides the poor with opportunities.

creating the capability

De Beers and Iscor have set up offices in India. Pharmaceutical, machinery and general trading companies are returning the compliment. Representatives of India's two million exporters fill the planes every week. Powerful Indian families on both sides of the ocean wait for the rest of us to test the water.

At the moment there is more talk than action. Downtown shops make South Africans suspicious of the Indian trader; quality and ethics are questioned. Indian companies that want to do business here will have to change perceptions, otherwise million-rand deals will be lost because the customer once bought a Gucci silk tie that was actually Fordsburg polyester.

As the Indian business community establishes its credentials, so South Africans can make their first exploratory steps without leaving home. Many of the new Indian businessmen coming to South Africa are world travellers. They know what India has and what it lacks. Two-way trade starts with the exchange of information and trust.

Indian business is also active on the Internet, with daily offerings that range from buyers wanting a million metric tons of fertiliser and 300 000 tons of sugar to sellers offering a million tons of wheat and rice; from joint ventures for a multinational courier service and the establishment of a brewery in Bangalore to manufacturing perfumery chemicals and operating a cell phone network.

A trip to India is potentially more enlightening and profitable than the usual America, Europe or Far East jaunt. There we are marginal customers and suppliers. In India we may find our destiny.

The poor in southern Africa and India draw us together. The world has profited from both subcontinents long enough. It is time to reach across the ocean that joins us; not to take from each other, but to give and to grow.

'Whenever you are in doubt or when the self becomes too much with you, apply the following test.

Recall the face of the poorest and the weakest man you may have seen and ask yourself if the step you contemplate is going to be of any use to him.

Will he gain anything by it? Will it restore him to a control over his own life and destiny? Then you will find your doubts and your self melting away.' MAHATMA GANDHI

four
three-wheeling through Africa

The wheels of fortune

You hear the music from five blocks away. Then a voice as deep as Barry White's rumbles 'Napoli, Napoli', and you feel the vibrations through the pavement. Next it's the turn of the gospel-tinged Sounds of Blackness, richly harmonising with 'Napoli, Napoli'.

When the three-wheeler comes into view, you see macro-graphics of temptingly cool ice-creams and lollies. Suddenly the day is hotter, your mouth is drier and that small change in your pocket is itching to be spent.

Napoli is the funkiest fleet of ice-cream vans in Africa. They are part of our growing street theatre, and their gelatis taste every bit as Italian as a glass of chilled chianti.

Now stockbrokers are discreetly humming the catchy Napoli jingle. Could the time for a share listing be near? The six partners are keeping their options open. The business is debt-free, and multinationals have been paying it attention.

Napoli operates as a franchise that has enabled 3 000 mini-entrepreneurs to start their own businesses. The partners, who began with 10 three-wheelers and an old ice-cream factory in Durban eight years ago, attribute their success to the mode of delivery.

Imported from India, the Bajaj three-wheelers cost one-third of the amount of locally made bakkies. They are economical and easy to maintain.

Lower transport costs allow Napoli to price their ice-creams 20 per cent below those of the competition, as well as turn their small vans into mobile music billboards.

'Napoli, Napoli.' Now it's the sweet soul of missjones. The music keeps the three wheels of fortune rolling.

Business Africa, May 2004

For one-third of the price of a local bakkie, you can buy an imported three-wheeler. There are half-tonners, three-quarter tonners and taxis that take three passengers. They are powered by 150 cc, two-stroke, air-cooled engines.

The taxi cruises along quite happily at 65 kilometres per hour and can do between 25 and 40 kilometres on one litre of petrol, giving it a range of up to 300 kilometres. The pick-up and delivery vans have a 50 kilometre-per-hour top speed. And they are as easy to maintain as an electric lawnmower.

Three-wheelers helped to re-establish Italy's economy after the Second World War. They have empowered millions in the Far East and have made an ice-cream manufacturer from Chile a multi-millionaire.

Over one million are sold around the developing world each year.

The 'General Motors' of three-wheelers is Bajaj in India. In May 1994, Bajaj South Africa opened for business.

the roads of southern africa

It is easier to drive from two remote villages in the Drakensburg to Johannesburg than from one of these villages to the other. South African roads and transport are geared to inter-district rather than intra-district travel.

Our trucks, buses, taxis and trains ignore township realities such as relatively short distances, poor roads (if any) and poverty.

Bajaj three-wheelers are built for rutted roads, crowded places and the low incomes of India. They trade unwanted speed and unnecessary frills for practicality, reliability and economy.

Yet they are hardly ever stolen because they are not ideal getaway vehicles.

creating micro-businesses

We guarantee your three-wheeler loan with the bank. We give you business training. And we pay for two advertisements on your van. All you need are good references and a motor-cycle licence.

It means your three-wheeler can cost you less than R350 a month. And you're a mobile spaza shop. You sell whatever you like. Except when it comes to washing powder. Only our brands, please.

There are more than 100 townships of over 100 000 people each that have no supermarkets and very few cafés. They have spazas that charge up to 40 per cent more than shops in the suburbs for a soft drink or floor polish.

Most spaza owners own little more than a wobbly bicycle. They must pay for transport to town, then negotiate with café owners for a discount.

Three-wheelers allow many more people to own commercial transport. By becoming mobile wholesalers for spaza shops and convenient retailers for the public, three-wheelers bring reliable deliveries and lower prices to communities with the most need. Corporations can assist in the creation of micro-businesses, while they gain a strategic advantage by opening new channels of distribution.

How do you take an egg stain off a silk shirt?
What's the new shampoo for straightened hair?
Come to Mr Kleen, the three-wheeler shop with all
the cleaning products and advice you want.
Just look for the green, fibreglass

Mr Kleen
on the roof of our vans.

---

carry the window frames to extension three

From squatter shacks to mansions in the northern suburbs, people are building and upgrading a million homes. They are buying wood, doors, window-frames, geysers and Italian tiles from building merchants, discounters and cash-and-carry stores.

But who wants to carry two window-frames four kilometres to Extension Three? Who wants to be seen in a Mercedes full of bricks?

Three-wheeler bakkies are low-cost pick-up and delivery vehicles. From truck tyres to gas-tanks, from watermelons to cement, they connect local businesses with the people they serve.

Some of these goods carriers will be owned by retailers; others will be independents who wait for business outside Cashbuild, Dions and the farmers' co-operative.

the fashion wagons

Major fashion stores don't want to turn their floors into permanent bazaars by selling outdated ranges and left-over stock at a discount. Factory shops want hawkers to walk out with a vanful rather than an armful of goods. Low-cost importers are looking for new markets.

Many kilometres away, the millions who live in semi-urban townships and rural communities take pride in the way they dress.

Three-wheeler fashion wagons bridge the gap, travelling to different townships on market days, parking by churches, community centres and railway stations. If one place isn't prime, the fashion wagon moves on. The three rules of retailing: 'position, position and position' are replaced by 'mobility, mobility and mobility'.

Expect niche fashion wagons such as 'Babeez', 'Fashion-Tees' and 'Large and Lovely'. Brightly painted three-wheelers called 'Egg-Hedz' will offer school clothes, books and stationery at budget prices. 'Shoes on Wheels' bring Nike, North Star, Bruno Magli and community-made sandals to millions of potential customers.

These fashion wagons can create a new distribution system of warehouse shops situated at rural and urban crossroads. The front of the shop is a retail outlet, while at the back the three-wheelers load up.

fast food

The 'Hot Box' is a design for a restaurant on three wheels. It has a deep-fryer, a food-warming compartment, a cooler box, storage and display cabinets, a fold-out table and a well-displayed menu.

Individuals will buy or rent Hot Boxes to sell Indian and Chinese food, fish and chips, chicken, burgers and boerewors rolls outside shopping malls, on main streets, at railway stations, at industrial sites and at sports events.

After mobile food pioneers have blazed the trail, the franchise opportunities will increase. Expect 'The Hurry Curry', 'Burger-A-Go-Go', 'Chicken Van', 'The Flying Fish', 'The Sandwich Car' and 'Papmobile'.

Good Food Guides will include a 'Three-wheeler – What's hot and what's not' section written by roving critics: ' ... while Samoosa Heaven is a slight, yet pardonable, exaggeration, the Guguletu Hurry Curry was renamed the 'Hara-Kiri' by a party of indisposed businessmen from Kyoto.'

take an open-air taxi

They have three wheels, three seats in the back, open sides and a detachable canvas roof. Their operators give tourists a guided tour of the waterfront, ferry hotel guests to beaches and take shoppers up and down busy streets. Autorikshas have a holiday feeling that conventional taxis just cannot match.

The millions of tourists that will visit South Africa create opportunities for thousands of autoriksha owner-drivers. The Autoriksha Association will advise members on driver courtesy and all business matters. Autorikshas will never be the fastest taxis around, but they could become the fastest selling.

At present Waterfront authorities have not sanctioned autorikshas as they want their taxis to carry more than three people. Whether this is the view of the authorities, taxi-driver associations or potential customers is unclear, but if we don't try, we'll never know.

three-wheeling through africa

Southern Africa is natural territory for three-wheelers. As peace and democracy spread through our subcontinent, the apostles of African capitalism could follow, riding their three-wheelers into even the most shattered communities, building hope for a better life.

We may soon be assembling three-wheelers in southern Africa. Manufacturing is less likely as the Indian factories are state of the science, with welding robots and automatic painting lines – unless we can make a technological leap.

Eskom has already designed an electric sports car. An environmentally friendly electric three-wheeler should not pose a problem. A solar-powered version is being made in Hawaii and sold in Japan. Using the sun to connect communities is an African solution. Electric or solar, three-wheelers would unchoke Bangkok, the world centre of auto-pollution, make the West less dependent on the oil pool, and allow this continent to develop in a cleaner, quieter way.

But virtue alone is rarely a winning formula. Three-wheelers have to become sexy. Wait for designs by Ferrari, Esteé Lauder and Levi Strauss: the Ladyhawker in shocking pink, the Ricksha-Roller with leather seats and the Three-Graffee covered in hand-sprayed messages.

Zinkwazi Retirement Village

On the beautiful Dolphin Coast, 15 minutes from airport
Tennis courts, indoor and outdoor pools and bowls
Two restaurants, bar and frail-care facilities
Fishing boat and fleet of ultra-quiet sola-rikshas for residents' use
Tel: 084 837 2222

---

three-wheeler update

BP and Caltex are now experimenting with Bajaj three-wheelers to sell paraffin in the townships. The University of Namibia is using them for ground maintenance and the Overburg Municipality recently bought some for their cleaning staff to reach far-flung holiday chalets. A South African ice-cream company is conducting a feasibility study, and three-wheelers are about to be used for a mobile car-wash franchise that visits car parks.

Banks have been reluctant to finance three-wheelers for two reasons. The first, ironically, is because they are inexpensive. The same paperwork is needed for an R18 500 Bajaj as a R500 000 Ferrari, making the Bajaj a relatively unprofitable transaction. The second is that the applicant, an aspirant entrepreneur, usually has no credit track record. If of course the applicant offers a sizeable deposit, the transaction becomes even more unprofitable for the bank.

Entrepreneurs need finance and there are huge opportunities awaiting banks that re-engineer themselves to encourage small and micro-business. It is the subject of the next chapter.

Be environmentally friendly.
Call Glass-Go to collect all your
empty wine bottles, jars and broken glass.
Recycling helps us all!

Glass-Go
The City Rangers
Tel: 084 909 7321

five
can you make money out of the poor?

The banking table

As the boys in the village herd the cows away, the women bring the banking table out of the hut that is the store and set it down in the shade of the waterberry tree. Three women ferry a dozen chairs from the hut, while a fourth polishes the table. We are in the rolling, green hills of Zululand between Rourke's Drift and Tugela Ferry. This is still a rural area although the villages are bigger than they were in the past. And to this village, the banker comes every Wednesday.

People from surrounding villages stand in three queues. The banker arrives in her bakkie at 8:30 a.m. She takes out her briefcase, lays it on the table, then walks over to greet the seated elders. At 8:50 a.m. the chief walks from his hut to the chair behind the table. The banker walks to the chair next to his. They clasp hands then sit down. The bank is about to open.

The queue on the left is made up of loan-seekers. The queue in the middle, in front of the banker, is made up of savers. The queue on the right, in front of the chief, is made up of loan-seekers approved by him. The banker takes out a small pile of money from the computer briefcase and places it on a table. She flips up a minisatellite dish and the chief ceremoniously logs on.

Savers start to deposit money. Then, as the float grows, the first chief-approved loan is processed. If any money remains by the time the chief's queue is satisfied, borrowers from the left-hand queue will benefit.

Although the bank has just opened, a stir of expectancy ripples through the left-hand queue. The banker's pile of cash is larger than last week and the line of savers is longer. New homes will be built because of today, and new businesses started. One woman in the queue, with exquisitely braided hair, does not join in the buzz around her. She looks over to where the chief sits. He looks in her direction and turns away ...

It is time banks recognise and address the true needs of all South Africans. If they continue to favour the economically empowered, they will throw fuel into a smouldering fire.

Yet banks have a fiduciary duty to protect their savers' money. And they must provide an acceptable rate of return to their investors. A bank is a symbol of security and trust. Conscience can never be allowed to overpower prudence. While the exclusivity of the banking system could lead to revolution, its collapse would lead to anarchy.

Banks cannot continue operating as they have been doing for many decades, nor can they give up what they represent.

do banks need bricks and mortar?

In South Africa, many large communities have no bank. Smaller communities will have to wait a lifetime for local access if a traditional branch has to be built.

Bricks and mortar raise the cost of starting a bank. For this reason, not enough banks have been built until now. Yet there are barefoot bankers in India and bankers on bicycles throughout Bangladesh. Bankers sat in the souks and the bazaars of Casablanca and Istanbul; the Rothschilds began as money lenders in the street-market of Frankfurt.

In the future, bricks and mortar will be an option for South African banks, not a limitation. The hawkers' bank operates out of converted containers, and Community Bank is looking at on-line containers equipped with satellite dishes. Meanwhile, personal computers bring banking into the office and home.

Bankers can now be represented by machines and maintaining an ATM costs far less than maintaining a branch. Whilst many financial institutions are taking this option and something is better than nothing, bankers are beginning to realise that a machine does not inspire loyalty. Since banks have been putting ATMs on suburban high streets, retailers have welcomed shoppers into their stores with customer-friendly banking services. If bankers want to build brand-loyalty as well as their business amongst the unbanked, they need a more hands-on approach. They can rent a room in the township community hall, share premises with the local builder's merchant or set up a stall in the local market, doing business where business is done.

Ask communities what they would most like from a bank and they will answer: 'To be here'.

micro-enterprise before housing

Communities also put small-business loans before home loans. Townships were built as dormitory towns with no provision for trade or business. They remain impoverished because money pours out of them. Micro-enterprises can plug many leaks. As more flourish and trade with the outside world as well as with each other, they become wealth creators for the whole community.

There are 2,5 million micro-enterprises in South Africa employing more than four million people. Forty per cent of these are hawkers who need to borrow the cost of their stock so that they can buy at the best wholesale prices. Achib is the hawkers' association that now runs banks out of converted containers donated by Safmarine. Hawkers are lent money at the rate of one per cent a day. You borrow R100 in the morning, buy and sell your merchandise, and then pay back R101 in the evening. Achib also issues you a card that enables you to buy wholesale at major cash-and-carry outlets.

The interest rate, which is the equivalent of over 300 per cent a year, simply isn't an issue. The hawkers' bank enables the poor to be self-employed. They are mainly women; men are far more likely to spend the R100 loan on other things.

Around the world, corporations shed people while small enterprises are growing. The informal sector in South Africa shows that entrepreneurial spirit exists throughout our society. Many of the micro-enterprises are run by survivalists — men and women who sell oranges on the pavements because they cannot find a job. Some of these businesses however have been started by emergent entrepreneurs. Banks that can identify these job-makers of tomorrow and help them with start-up loans will mobilise the savings of the community for the good of that community. One hand will wash the other.

can you make money out of the poor?

The Bank Rakyat Indonesia has 45 000 employees. Half of them work in the informal sector and provide two-thirds of the bank's profits. There are 4 000 units in villages and each is a profit centre. A new unit is expected to break even within 18 months, and then the staff will share one per cent of the profits. Millions of hawkers, one- or two-people factories and local builders have been empowered. Is it a coincidence that building costs per square metre in Indonesia are a third of South African costs?

The Grameen Bank of Bangladesh, started by Dr Muhammad Aeneas with a $30 loan in 1976, now has 1 000 branches serving more than two million people. The average loan is under $70, and 98 per cent of all loans are repaid. It is usually uneconomical to grant loans like these, as even the simplest credit check would cost more than the interest received, and very few landless Bangladeshi peasants are listed by credit bureaux.

Grameen's strategy is peer lending. To obtain a loan, an individual must band together with four neighbours. The group meets with the loan officer and chooses one or two of themselves to be eligible for a loan. Before anyone else can receive a loan, the first members have to make regular repayments. Peer pressure is far stronger than a banker's letter. And more economical.

Ninety-two per cent of Grameen's clients are women who want to start their own businesses. An initial loan of $40 is enough for a grocery stall, to buy seeds for a crop or bamboo for stools.

The bank is more than a provider of money. Clients are trained in nutrition, hygiene, child care, birth control, and basic agricultural and handicraft economics. Their group physical exercises, slogan chanting and ritualised greetings are seen as excessive by some outsiders. However, it creates an environment that, despite the huge pressure of tradition, allows rural Bangladeshi women to empower themselves. The Grameen strategies are working; 48% of those who have borrowed from the bank for ten years have crossed the poverty line and another 27% have neared it.

Informal banking initiatives in Zimbabwe were also supported mainly by women. Rural men here, as everywhere else in the world, seem to be less reliable and show less initiative in starting something new.

In South Africa, various initiatives like Community Bank and NuBank have been set up to reach poorer communities. Institutions like Theta are specialising in micro-lending, as are many organisations that are of dubious provenance. Go to any small town in South Africa and you will see more money-lenders than furniture stores. They extend credit so people can buy bread, charge usurious rates, and then encourage their customers to re-finance debt. They flourish in the absence of responsible micro-lenders, fulfilling a need in the short term while creating debt traps that will financially ruin thousands of families later on.

If banks do not provide an alternative, the money-lenders will create more poverty. Meanwhile, the rural areas continue to subsist outside the banking system. Thirteen million people, mostly young and poor, live in rural South Africa; and the numbers are growing. Maybe the solution can be found in the words of Dr Muhammad Aeneas, founder of the Grameen Bank in Bangladesh:

> *'If we are looking for one single action that will enable the poor to overcome their poverty, I would go for credit. Money is power. I have been trying to make the world accept and treat credit as a basic human right.'*

Although South Africa has millions of poor people, it does not have the levels of poverty seen in Somalia, Bangladesh and India. And we do have world-class financial institutions. It seems logical that this country should be a leader in banking for the unbanked, rather than a reluctant also-ran.

show me how

South Africa's core need: human development

How a bank can deliver: training – information – networking – mobilising savings – financing – money management

If a bank could see human development as its mission, it could unlock the potential of millions across Africa – and discover significant new sources of revenue.

'I know how to build, but I don't know how to manage the project. I don't know how to charge, how to keep my books, how to make my cash flow better. Teach me the business of building. Show me how, please.' JOEL S

Builders, spaza owners, and dressmakers are all looking for some form of business training – and banks seek to protect the money they lend. 'Help your customers be better customers' is a sound business principle. Cautious bankers can put preconditions on loans: 'Take the training course, establish a savings track record with us, and you can have the money you need.' Lenders pay for the training with slightly higher or extra installments.

Everyone wins. The entrepreneur is given help that is vital to her success and, as a result, access to finance. The bank makes an early convert and creates a new source of income while its loans are more secure.

The community is the prime benefactor. Builders trained in project management can deliver more houses more cost effectively. Hawkers know how to contain costs, while spazas can upgrade, buy better products and merchandise more effectively.

A training and learning bank benefits from the two most effective forms of advertising: word of mouth and successful case histories.

from banks to brands

Bangladeshi village women embroidering bed covers destined for the big cities and export now call their clients on cell phones when they are ready. Thanks to Grameen Telecom, an offshoot of Grameen Bank, the rural poor of Bangladesh have affordable communications as well as credit. One project, the Village Pay Phone (VPP), will reach out to millions of the world's poorest people. Selected borrowers of the Grameen Bank will lease the phone and make it available to all villagers, undertake short message services and enable others to receive incoming calls. VPP is likely to become the largest wireless pay phone project in the world and it is made possible through a reliable network of micro-lenders and the trusted brand of Grameen.

Once you are doing business with the poor, and making sincere efforts to help them escape their poverty, you are building loyalty to your brand that can be leveraged beyond traditional banking products. The banking group that establishes itself in South African rural areas today could sell cell phones, computers, internet access, training and educational processes tomorrow. The brand name could extend to recruitment services and business centres, providing opportunities and information to those who need it most. Banks spend hundreds of millions of rands on communicating their brand values. A little less 'say' and a little more 'do' could be the best investment in their brand that they have ever made. By addressing the true needs of all South Africans banks can do well.

Most of the people in the three queues in front of the banker's table are women. Some are saving for homes; some want sewing machines to start a co-operative clothing business. One wants a loom to weave tapestries for tourists, and two who have grocery stalls need finance for stock.

The woman with the exquisitely braided hair is one of the chief's wives. She wants to open a hairdressing salon, but as the chief does not approve she must wait in the left-hand queue. Now that the sun is high, the queues have dwindled and the banker's pile remains, it is her turn to approach.

The banker and the chief confer. 'What troubles you, sir?' the banker asks.

'I have questioned myself a thousand times. I have questioned my councillors. And still I don't know. Is it right for a chief's wife to work for others?'

'I think this question only the chief's wife can answer,' the banker replies.

The chief is silent for a minute. Then he stands and walks across to his wife.

'I believe you are in the wrong queue,' he says, and leads her over to his side. The banker counts out the money for the loan. She then enters it on-line to the group's central data-bank. The green light in the mini satellite dish glows and the chime from the computer signals the receipt of the transaction.

Horizons, February 2008

SIX
what can you do with dirt?

Ukuphupha People's Radio rides the waves!

'This is a pa-aa-arty ... and I want you to celebrate now ... this is your time ... Ukuphupha ... this is your voice ... this is the beginning, for I have the honour to declare Ukuphupha People's Radio well and truly launched ... may you ride high on the airwaves ... Ukuphupha, this is your time to dance!'

The crowded market explodes in cheers and ululations, flower sellers throw bouquets in the air as the Layzee Boyz appear to mime their latest hit single. Barbers snip and style, sangomas throw the bones, fresh vegetables are weighed, pap is heated, trinkets bargained for and clothes tried on.

The market pauses to celebrate the opening of the radio station and the visit of the DJ from Johannesburg, but the beat doesn't stop. You can buy almost anything here, from the latest hemp jackets to the best milktart in Mpumalanga.

'The Layzee Boyz, my honeys and bunnies. Give them an Ukuphupha welcome!'

Through the cheers he says softly into the microphone: 'You guys are something else. You're turning dirt into gold.'

Community Talk, March 2006

There are many townships out of the media spotlight. This one we can call Ukuphupha, the Zulu word for 'dream'. It is in Mpumalanga along the N12 motorway. Over 100 000 people live there, with

what can you do with dirt?

perhaps 50 000 more on surrounding farms. Few, even those who drive past, have heard of it.

The region's economy rests on agriculture (mealies, potatoes, beans and chickens), coal-mining and power stations. The area, in terms of acid rain, is the third most polluted in the world. There is 40 per cent unemployment, while many of those with jobs earn only survival wages.

In the dusty main street there are a couple of cafés, a butcher, a bottle-store and a beer hall. Along every road are spazas and hairdressers. There are a few taxis and a couple of coal-yards in the squatter camp.

There are no supermarkets or clothing stores, yet there are 10 000 schoolchildren in the township who must go to town to buy a school uniform. And there is no bank, while the small town supports three.

The township is calm. There are no broken windows in the schools and no gunshots at night. Homes range from shacks recently visited by typhoid to matchbox constructions and a few brick houses with carports.

It is a site and services area. I saw a family on an empty site with their possessions surrounding them. An old man and woman sat on a faded sofa. The elder grandchildren stood around uncertainly while the younger ones played hide-and-seek among the belongings.

'The parents and their friends are out finding building materials. By tonight they will have a roof over their heads,' Alan said as we drove past. There would be no bankers involved in the transaction, no bonds or records. They would simply pay the 'ezinc' man for some basic materials.

Two weeks later I went back along the same street. Which corrugated iron home was theirs? I couldn't tell.

The summer rains were still two months off the first time I visited, and the fields on the way were the colour of winter gold. In Ukuphupha there was hardly a blade of grass. As we drove the seven kilometres from the township into the town, we passed the nine-hole golf-course. Many of its greens, although patchy, were still green.

Some time later, I was talking to a friend about the place and asked: 'How can Ukuphupha escape its poverty trap?'

'Open a casino,' he replied with a smile.

I must have turned up my puritan nose a bit. He gave a helpless kind of shrug. 'What else can you do with dirt?'

45

capacity building

The process has already begun. Organisations like the Independent Development Trust send their capacity builders into townships to help set up structures. Once trust is gained within the community, a development association is started. A leader is chosen, and then a phone, fax machine and meeting-place are organised.

The development association forms committees that deal with job creation, housing, health, education, sport, recreation and the environment. The leader is sent on training courses and regular meetings are scheduled to carry the process forward.

Capacity building is preparing for future growth; channels must be dug before the rains. Early tasks include identifying possible leaders and developing their potential. A man trained to blow up troop carriers (and did it well) becomes a committed leader of reconciliation and reconstruction in his community, building bridges of trust between his sprawling township and the small, nervous white town just down the road, with its banks, garages, high street of shops, golf-course, gyms and floodlit rugby field.

Capacity building is putting negotiating structures in place. Nothing can be taken for granted. Some members of a development association told me about their first 18 months: 'Many of our people are expecting everything to happen overnight. They are not happy with the progress. They do not understand many things. We must teach people what a government is, and the nature of interaction between leaders and followers.'

Each community travels at its own pace, depending on the leaders, the spirit in the township and the ability of the capacity builders. Some find consensus quickly while others are mired in constant dispute. On the emotional agenda are poverty, anger, disease, fear, mistrust, expectation and disappointment. The development association meetings often have a directness that is lacking in most boardrooms.

'I apologise to the meeting for not having a written report of the project. We were very busy and had a record month.'

'I do not think we can accept this apology. Firstly, the written report is necessary to tell us how the project workers feel. Secondly, if the project leader has not written the report, he may need some help. But how can we help him until he asks for it?'

what can you do with dirt?

In the boardroom: 'You haven't written the report? Don't worry about it.' Then leaning over to whisper 'Bloody fool' behind a hand.

Capacity building can be compared to a water jug. It may be strong and have a pleasing design – but you still need the water to fill it.

the sieve and the circuit

Townships are like sieves – money pours out of them. If you want to buy any groceries beyond the limited and pricey selection at the spaza shop, if you want new clothes, your shoes repaired, or to collect your pension from the bank, you must travel to town. It will cost at least R2 by taxi to go there and back. And in rural townships a rand is still a rand. Women collect large bundles of firewood that they sell for R1 each.

As money pours out, the township remains in poverty. The sieve has to be replaced by the circuit, which encourages money to go around. The faster it travels, the better off residents will be. The amount of money is less important than the velocity of it.

The simplest and least expensive way to set up the circuit is to open a market, a central area where things are made and traded. As the market is a gathering place, it creates a demand for food, groceries, clothes, building materials, services like banking and shoe repairs, as well as entertainment. The demand will create the supply and the loop will be closed.

A market is a gathering of people where news and gossip are traded as much as clothes and food. Industry hives separate the makers from the sellers. They are rarely in the right places for trade and are not customer friendly. These hives may make sense on drawing boards, but they are not natural. Imposed solutions rarely work, and too often the blame for the failure is laid at the doors of the people upon whom these solutions were imposed. Before we go forward, we should look back.

history, fleas and the italian spine

Markets are not a new idea. They answer a basic human need that says: 'I am not self-sufficient. I can do this well, but I can't do that. I'd like to trade with you.' Farmers' markets create towns and port markets create cities. All over the world and throughout history – from caveman to cyberspace – markets have created communities.

If a market doesn't exist, a community has to invent one. Flea markets are sprouting up in the concrete. There are instant waterfronts and organic farmers in suburbia, rows of food stalls and pavement barbers by the bus depots in town.

We all need the 'high-touch', the personal attention, that shopping malls, supermarkets and catalogues cannot provide. People in flea markets talk to each other. There's music, food and laughter, as well as business. Flea markets take in over $7 billion in Australia. In South Africa, they sell more T-shirts than any chain-store. Flea markets have been grafted onto an urban, mall-filled landscape, and they work. In their natural environment, they blossom.

Along the hilly spine of Italy, especially towards the north, there are many quietly prosperous villages. In the heart of each is the market that bursts into life on market day. The villages are connected by hawkers and traders who have an established route. With them travel the entertainers. On market day there are streamers, magic, music, food and dancing. People come from surrounding farms to buy, sell and be entertained. They share the latest gossip, and in the taverns that night they hear the news from other villages.

Traders travelling along the spine of Italy bring markets and villages to life. African markets are full of colour and excitement – like the clothes and spice markets of Ghana, or the fabled night markets of Benin, lit by swaying kerosene lamps, where people travel a hundred miles to find a bargain, meet old friends, listen to the flutes, make some money and see the magicians start fires in mud, walk on water, or cause rice to rain from the sky.

In Malawi, the traders are gathered in a central square, while around them the tailors and dressmakers sit outside with their sewing machines on the patios of their homes, ready to make a black skirt or blue shirt, depending on demand. Just in time production may have been re-invented by Japanese industry, but like much else it began in the markets.

starting a market

Thanks to the apartheid planners, who liked to leave big spaces in townships for tanks to roll through and gather, South Africa has built

what can you do with dirt?

up urban areas with central land ready-made for markets. You will find a township with Extension Two on one side, Extension Three on another and Extension Four somewhere else. There's open ground in the middle. It's a perfect meeting point.

The market can begin with a collection of hawkers, tailors, cobblers, mealie-meal grinders, vegetable growers and farmers.

While they don't need a shopping mall over their heads, some structure would help their enterprise. Enough has to be happening to attract a number of people. A market needs a critical mass.

Dr Norman Reynolds of the Market Society believes a people's market should have these ingredients:

- a fenced area; water, toilets, electricity and public telephones
- various spaces for trade, either shaded or covered (for instance, thatch roofs on split poles)
- an area for traders to park their vehicles, from which they can sell
- workshops for grinding mills, knitters, and cobblers
- a bank, pension service, library and clinic
- a safe store building and an office
- a crèche
- crop collection facilities, a livestock yard and an auction market
- cooking and food selling
- a laundry and baker
- an open-air auditorium and a performing-arts shed.

A performance shed looks like a barn; it is simple and user-friendly. Most community centres are the wrong shape, volume and height for performances. They also cost too much. A performance shed is part of the atmosphere, with a wide verandah for trading and entertainment on market day. It hosts art, dancing, choirs, musical groups, boxing, movies, plays, meetings and parties.

Trade and culture come together at a market. It is a celebration and sharing of community skills. Some people grow mealies, some play music; all have something to offer and all are valued. (In Johannesburg, the Market Theatre was once a produce market. Now the theatre is supported by rents from its flea market. And so the wheel turns ...)

The market's safe storage facilities and offices can be home to the farmers' union, the development association and a bank-sponsored video training scheme. The crèche is open to all.

Building a market and performance shed is not a million-rand, 16-signature project. A dozen market rings would cost less than a modest shopping mall. And of course, rentals would be lower, allowing the disadvantaged to set up shop.

The development association will bring the community into the process. It will be their market, inspired by their design and charge rentals they believe are fair. The developers will probably not make a profit from the stall owners in the early years, and so they should consider sponsorship with the offer of naming rights.

Poster advertising can cover maintenance costs, while the performance shed may enjoy its own sponsorship.

Tonight at the Toyota Showhouse:
New Talent Night
Tomorrow:
The City Dancers in their hit production
From Tiekiedraai to Toyi-Toyi

Rural areas need a ring of markets linked by travelling hawkers. Seven markets can cover an area housing half a million people, giving a market day to each community and full-time employment for the sellers as well as local makers, whose goods can now reach far more people. Opportunities exist to establish a centralised trade house serving each market ring. It will act as a wholesaler, as well as a buyer of local goods for 'export' to the cities. Each trade house can also contain a micro-business bank.

Urban townships may not need the ring of markets, but they will be made more exciting by the variety and news that travelling hawkers bring. Bigger markets will become popular destinations as they build up a reputation for their food, their flowers or their Saturday morning boxing tournaments.

what can you do with dirt?

A market will not bring instant riches to an impoverished area. It is a spark, not the flame. It can be a wealth-builder, a community-maker, a place of intrigue, information and fun where everyone will win – at least some of the time. Container-cities will develop, and so one day may the shopping mall. But you don't need a Mercedes to benefit from wheels.

ukuphupha update

During 1995, a ring of seven markets started around Stutterheim in the Eastern Cape. Another ring began around Sekhukhuneland in the Northern Province and a third ring is operating south of Mafikeng. The seed money came from Great Britain; in South Africa we are too busy building shopping malls.

The Market Society is now involved in two massive urban projects, both in Gauteng. One is to build markets in the East Rand townships that became war-zones in the struggle for freedom, and the other is to relocate Johannesburg's inner city hawkers from the streets to covered areas that will feature sought-after amenities like bath-houses. A key part of the plan is to encourage and train hawkers to be more diverse in the goods and services that they offer.

There is a market sub-committee for the township I have called Ukuphupha. But as yet there is no market. Corporations look at the possibilities and do their balancing act. What comes first, a school or a market? Water or a market? A highly publicised football match or a market? Only a market creates sustainable employment, but it needs to be done properly for it to become the focal point of an area and a destination that makes people either turn off the motorway or wake up early to hitch a ride.

There is no market in Ukuphupha. Potential donors and business people come to the township, spend an hour or two, then shake the red earth from their shoes and speed back to the city of gold, listening to Phil Collins sing 'Another day in Paradise' while Ukuphupha goes back to its dreams.

seven
better than money

Fat cat burglar given stick

There is a new weapon in the war against crime, a Chiswick Crown Court was told yesterday. The weapon is legal, practical and pleasing to the eye. It is a hand-carved ebony walking-stick from Africa — now also known as the 'Malawi Stop-Nonsense'.

Witness to the power of this new, or rather traditional, weapon is Mr Bill Potter, an unsuccessful cat burglar who appeared in court yesterday with a large bandage wrapped around his head. While attempting to enter the garden flat of Miss Penny Sinton through the dining-room window, the overweight Mr Potter became stuck.

Hearing strange rattles and grunts, Miss Sinton armed herself with an ebony walking-stick she had recently bought then walked into the dining-room.

There she saw Mr Potter trying to wiggle through the half-open window. She stepped up, steadied herself and, with an arm action honed by years of club tennis, knocked him out with a single blow. Miss Sinton phoned the police and the still dazed Mr Potter was taken into custody.

At yesterday's court hearing, Judge Wilkins asked the accused to take off his bandage and noted that the bump was the size of a large egg. Then she asked to see the walking-stick that had been presented in evidence. Creatures from African myths were carved into the dark, glowing wood.

After giving a few practice swings, Judge Wilkins enquired as to whether the walking-stick was also known as the 'Malawi Stop-Nonsense'. The prosecutor confirmed that it was.

The judge commended Miss Sinton for doing her civic duty, then regarded Mr Potter's lump again, saying she was pleased it had put a stop to his nonsense. Bail was denied.

This unexpected publicity has delighted Tom Dumba of the African Barter Company, the importers of the walking-sticks. Dumba describes the 'Malawi Stop-Nonsense' as art with a purpose. It is more decorative than a baseball bat, causes less mess than a .45 and is less aggressive than a Doberman.

About 20 000 of these ebony, hand-carved sticks have been exported to Europe by the bartering arm of a South African-based multinational company. It traded them for T-shirts and jeans with rural communities in Malawi.

Over 10 000 sticks had been sold before the bandaged Mr Potter was brought before the judge. Now that the 'Malawi Stop-Nonsense' has been held up in a London court as a fine example of British justice, more people in rural Africa can look forward to being well clothed.

The Times, May 2009

The rebirth of barter as big business started in 1984. The Los Angeles Olympics was the first in modern times to make a profit, and part of the credit was attributed to the $116 million worth of bartered goods and services.

A few years later, in the decisive 'cola wars', Pepsi beat Coke to the Russian market by trading shiploads of soft syrup for Stolichnaya vodka.

Now, almost 250 000 American companies are bartering. They include 65 per cent of the Fortune 500. Amongst the big players are Xerox, Pan Am, Chrysler, Pizza Hut, Casio, 3M, General Electric, Playtex and Hilton Hotels. Individuals such as lawyers, teachers and building contractors barter too.

Business through bartering exchanges in America is worth $7 billion a year, with over 10 per cent annual growth. The total US

renaissance dawning

barter trade is far more; estimates reach $100 billion. It is also big business in Asia, where companies barter $70 billion to $90 billion worth of goods and services each year. The world is now on-line through Barter-Net and U-Barter, providing a global market 24 hours a day.

Meanwhile, barter is a traditional strength of southern African people. Farmers have been trading with hunters, and sangomas with shoemakers for thousands of years. *Lobola* is a ritual with deep meaning: while some question the morality and relevance of the bartered bride, most re-embrace their tradition.

the barter advantage

Barter allows you to buy retail with wholesale costs. It conserves cash while using your excess product or time.

Hotels buy computers in exchange for rooms, music teachers buy Kenya safaris for lessons and rice is swapped for tractors. Start-ups with more capacity than cash trade for office space, furniture and stationery.

South African companies will have the opportunity to make new alliances and do business with the emerging economies around us who have things to offer other than cash.

There is also an emotional satisfaction in the direct trading of the tangible; things you can touch, taste and smell.

bartering in communities

Some communities now print their own barter currency. They follow the example set by the rural community of Ithaca in the United States, who started printing 'hours' in the early 1990s, each one equal to an hour of work.

An Ithaca doctor, who has a receptionist, expensive equipment and a consulting room, may charge an 'hour' for a 15 minute visit, while a manicurist earns an 'hour' for 60 minutes' work.

These 'hours' are only valid within the community. Their printing is strictly limited to control inflation.

Local newspapers publish the names of all those who take part in the scheme, from student baby-sitters to artists. This makes bartering a way to advertise and encourage new business.

If the idea spreads to rural communities in southern Africa ...

... a hawker pays a knitter, who pays the spaza shop, who in turn uses 'hours' for an auto mechanic, who pays the local sangoma, who can then pay her bank charges. The bank uses the 'hours' to pay the cleaners and gardeners, who then pay the hawkers ...

Community barter-money keeps work within the community, creates local spirit and includes many left out of the monetary loop.

the bartering business

Four hundred exchanges in the United States enlist the aid of computer networks. These exchanges are profit-making enterprises, charging an annual membership fee and up to 15 per cent commission on each trade.

Members have a barter credit card. If you sell $10 000 worth of products to another member, you receive $10 000 in trade credit (minus commission) that you use to buy goods or services from other members.

The advantages are similar to community 'hours'. You tend to do business with other people and companies in the exchange. They tend to return the favour, giving you new customers as well as absorbing your excess inventory and time. If you have high mark-ups or spare capacity, bartering will improve your bottom line.

Although barter exchange companies declare their dealings to the taxman, many private deals escape attention.

According to the multinational exchanges, 'hot' barters include office space, hotel rooms, airline tickets and advertising.

Although bartering is part of southern Africa culture, it is not big business yet. Will an American company target us? Local corporations are more familiar with the terrain.

bartering today ... and tomorrow

Companies in South Africa barter informally every day. Restaurant meals are swapped for radio time, chocolates buy air tickets and cars are paid for in oil. As more entrepreneurs enter the market, bartering will become more common. A writer buys legal aid for the cost of a pamphlet, a hawker pays for taxi-rides with potatoes, a pregnant accountant does the books of a baby shop and a glazier accepts gym membership for sliding windows.

Big corporations call it countertrade, and in a world where there's a distrust of most currencies, exchanging things for things is on the rise. Tanzania can exchange mining exploration rights for food and education. Zimbabwe may receive training and factories for semi-precious stones, tobacco and carvings. And in South Africa we could counter-trade technology for water, beer for wheat, and coal for hydro-electric power.

A gorilla called Pepsi

Burundi is rebuilding its economy, partly thanks to a gorilla named Pepsi. Last year the African Bartering Company arranged the swap of tractors for naming rights of tagged gorillas.

Quarterly reports on the activities of Pepsi with annual photographs and videos are proudly circulated world-wide by the soft drink company.

'Pepsi is a great spokesperson, or should that be spokesbiped, for Pepsi-Cola,' says an industry analyst. 'So what if he doesn't drink the stuff; nor did Michael and Whitney.'

Johannesburg is the trading centre of southern Africa and can become a barter centre of the world: solar panels for rice; machine parts for mangoes; computers for prawns. The barter economy will grow between the moneyed and non-moneyed nations, brokered by the nation that intimately understands the cultures of wealth and poverty.

In many parts of our continent, barter is better than money. It should become a competitive advantage in our bid to stage world events like the 2006 football World Cup. One day it may even reach out to strike an inept cat burglar in a London flat.

eight
back to the land

The re-ruralisation of Africa

Is Gauteng losing its lustre? Sleek, young urbanites have been spotted packing Guccis, selling Cabriolets and taking a train to the middle of nowhere.

Many alight at a small station deep in the Northern Province. As the train pulls away, an old bakkie carries them off to a new life. They are the latest recruits to Commune Amandla that rests in a high valley on the northern edge of the Drakensburg mountains.

Founded by students and faculty members from the University of the North, with help from the South African Timber Federation who built the log cabins, they live by their words, 'the land can provide'.

Commune Amandla grows macadamia nuts, avocados and melons. Thanks to refugees from the Gauteng business world, marketing is a core competence and the brown paper bags sporting the commune logo are as much in demand as their contents.

Commune members are allowed to keep their previous life's possessions in their bank accounts, and they pay for their log cabins with their work. Everything the commune earns, over and above expenses and reserves, is shared equally. It is like the kibbutzim of Israel with an African twist.

Everyone works on the land. The agronomists, the bookkeepers, the marketers, the pack designers and the traders are all what they once were, but now part-time.

Bringing the land to life is the focus of each commune member.

'I was 24 when I joined Commune Amandla,' says Maggie. 'I was aimless; I had one friend and she emigrated. Now I feel close to half a dozen people and I have a huge family. We share our lives. My brother asked how I could give up so much by coming here. I told him all I gave up was anxiety, greed and loneliness.'

The rural population of South Africa is not diminishing. Between 1985 and 2010 an extra three million people will be living off the land, most of them young. This excludes the continuing waves of illegal immigrants. Altogether, the rural population could grow by 40 per cent in 25 years. In the same period, our urban population will more than double.

While we focus on the problems of urbanisation, we cannot ignore the other side of the coin. If we do not give hope to rural South Africans, many more will drown in the increasing urban flood. If we want to solve the squatter problems in Cape Town, we must look to address rural poverty in the Eastern Cape.

The land of sub-Saharan Africa can provide for all her people. It is time to mix new technologies with old wisdoms, modern science with traditional values.

from kibbutz israel to commune africa

The Israeli kibbutz spirit has inspired world youth. They came from five continents to work and live together; to show the war-shattered world a modern miracle built out of idealism, imagination and sheer hard work.

Today, there are fewer young people in the kibbutzim as the population in Israel and the Western world has aged. Noble visions fade with the passing years, and arthritic hands find it harder to pick oranges from sunrise to sunset. The future of the kibbutz is in question.

The average age of South Africans is almost half the age of Israelis. Kibbutz Israel passes the baton to Commune Africa.

... *Commune Amandla has become economically viable partly because of another Israeli idea — the paying, part-time kibbutznik. Among them are students from*

Europe taking time out from their books, African Americans in search of a spiritual home, and a group of Johannesburg divorcees looking for new meaning in life.

They each pay a monthly rental for the pleasure of working in the fields from sunrise to sunset, six days a week. They cook, wash up and join in the fun (if they have any energy left), that ranges from sing-alongs and Saturday night parties to art classes and philosophical debates.

What a variety of communes there can be throughout southern Africa. Buy robust table wines, goat's-milk cheese and handicrafts from the 'Wine and Song Group' near the mouth of the Olifantsfontein River in the Western Cape. The Magalies Farming Commune investigates intensive farming techniques for fruit and vegetables, as well as bottling its own low-cost spring water. 'Flowers of Africa' in Mpumalanga grows flowers that are exported around the world. The 'Piesang People' in Natal export branded bananas, at a premium, to the quality-hungry markets of Europe.

The rural population of southern Africa will find teachers on their doorstep who can show them how modest prosperity is attained. Electricity and a tap may save hours of labour but these have to be paid for. The new ruralites will demonstrate how to use time most productively. In return, the old ruralites can share their deep understanding of the land's ways.

Until now the choice has been stark: be poor in the country or take a chance in the city. Commune Africa can show a third way: The land is able to support its people.

the knitting kibbutz

Electricity is making rural areas low-cost attractive to light industry. You do not have to be near a city to make clothes or shoes. Knitting and sewing communes can be set up in alliance with major fashion retailers, builders and banks. From villages in India manufacturing high quality clothes at low cost to villages in Italy manufacturing fashion for Benetton, the models already exist.

They have up to 200 producers who are trained by retailers and financed by community banks. The communes are given constant work subject to ongoing quality controls, and are paid for the amount they produce.

Clothes made by people who own their businesses and live with their families, rather than those produced in anonymous downtown sweatshops, please the retailer as well as the wearer. Besides style, quality and value, the customer is being offered an emotional benefit.

Apart from making an ongoing contribution to rural communities, a knitting kibbutz makes good business sense. Costs should come down and Asian imports will have some decent competition.

When the retailer urgently needs an extra order of a fashion item, the communes will go out of their way to help. And they will be paid for their effort. Because they are self-employed, strikes are less likely. The buyer has empowered the supplier.

The more productive communities will utilise their skills and assets to make clothes and accessories for travelling hawkers. We may even create an export business. Close to the Kruger Park in a rural community near Bushbuckridge, hand-painted children's dresses are produced for sale in American stores.

> ... Commune Amandla accepts, at any one time, 50 to 70 young adults who are first offenders on counts of buying drugs and stealing cars. Instead of time spent in jail, many courts now consider a year in a commune more beneficial to the offenders and society.

> 'We work too hard to get into any more trouble,' says one such offender, 'and the other commune members make sure we stay straight. In two months though, I go back home. And I'll be on the streets again ... '

new age communes

The information highway is liberating designers, programmers, writers and the new shopkeepers of the 'Universal Mall'. We don't need skyscrapers to conduct business any more. Video conferencing replaces travelling hours, and small towns in places like the Karoo can be repopulated. Independent members of virtual teams will gather from around the world to work on projects in cyberspace, while they live where they find the best quality of life. Families will thrive away from the cities.

back to the land

In the twenty-first century, small towns offer healthy, relatively drug- and crime-free communities, complete with satellite dishes, cellular phones and interactive multimedia teaching. Once again, kids will play in local parks and ride bicycles up and down the street; no one need lock themselves in at night.

Families can make new friends on the Internet, in the coffee-shop, at the pool, the community hall and the pub. They won't need two cars, large bonds and all the latest Northern suburb trappings. They may earn less than some of their city cousins, but by spending less, they will be the ones going on an overseas holiday.

There are small towns throughout South Africa that are slowly dying. Properties cost less than a second-hand Citi Golf. Some could be repopulated by children of the Information Age; the mind-workers of the twenty-first century. And then, in a small space, a range of intelligent, interesting people will be gathered. Free from big-city fears and anxieties, could they create a new Florence or Sienna; the heart of the African renaissance?

the party strategy

Many people like to circulate when they go to a party. A less hectic way of meeting other guests is to occupy a strategic position and let the party come to you. With the inevitable growth of tourism here, a million rural South Africans will find themselves in exactly the right places.

Escape the high anxiety world.
Visit Sabona on the northern Zululand coast.
You'll reach the resort of thatched huts, tennis courts and pools
in a twin-engine plane or four-wheel drive.
Here you can fish, explore the wilder parts of the Kruger Park
and cross into Mozambique. You will feast on fresh crayfish,
select the best Cape wines, snorkel and laze in an unspoilt lagoon.
The hotel is staffed by the growing village of Sabona
which was formerly a sub-economic cluster of fishermen's huts.
Now you will find and enjoy a thriving community with a
developing infrastructure of fishing, farming and handicrafts.
Sabona – a world away from the world.
All major credit cards accepted.

productivity versus morality

Land reform continues to be a deeply divisive issue. Afrikaner and black farmers have a fierce, almost mystical attachment to the land, and the drastic racial imbalance of land distribution cannot be resolved to everyone's satisfaction. Black landless farmers claim their right to land through morality and history. White landowners rely on productivity and law.

We are not unique. Since the Second World War there have been land reform experiments throughout South East Asia, South America and Africa. Many have failed; a few have partially succeeded. Land reform models include state collectives, peasant collectives, individual and family freeholds, and seven- to 99-year leases.

The most spectacular failures occur when the political will is weak, as in India; when politics overrides tradition, as in China; or when political instability reverses the reform process, as in much of Latin America.

Gradual failures occur when the imposed solution has no cultural roots. The collectives throughout South America went against the individualistic nature of peasant farmers. Other failures are caused by land reform being unsupported by any training or follow-up.

Relative successes in Taiwan and Kenya indicate that breaking up big farms into small, profitable, privately-owned units with fair compensation is the best way to combine morality with productivity. Co-operatives are seen as transitional measures, or necessary for harsh and unfertile soils where collective effort is beneficial.

Israel is a unique case. Collectives there may have come about through necessity, yet they quickly achieved a moral light that was seen by the world. In South Africa we already have the spark. Ubuntu can give rural collectives their reason to come together and to thrive. The new clan will be made up of people with a common interest and belief: 'The land can provide'.

South African agriculture can be made up of a patchwork of large, small and collective farms helping each other with labour, ideas and finance. Land reform can tear this country apart or bring it together, depending on whether morality is used as a weapon to punish past wrongs or as a unifying force to improve life for everyone.

back to the land

Since 1994 two million hectares of land have been approved for transfer to the benefit of 400 000 people. Some say the process is too fast, many others say it is no way near fast enough. Farmworkers are still being summarily evicted from their homes; in many farms apartheid still rules; and farmers are being murdered at a gruesome rate. Until land ownership becomes more equitable, and the treatment of all more humane, the land will continue to lose those who can seed it.

the ebb and the flow

Electricity will come to 400 000 more homes each year. In a decade, 90 per cent of rural South Africans will have water in their village if not in their kitchens. But the scars of rural poverty will take far longer to fade. Big cities, shown without warts in TV soap operas and ads, still have their power to excite and entice.

Some rural communities will continue to balance on the edge of existence as the men go in search of wealth, leaving behind the women, the children and the old. At the same time, villages will be strengthened and communities formed with renewed energy and dreams. They will attract a cross-section of our rainbow nation, from disenchanted big-city dwellers to villagers and farmers who discover they do not need to leave their ancestral homes to find their place of gold.

... 'Twenty years ... two million settlers!' is the aim of Commune Africa. Will the target of two million resettled urbanites in rural sub-Sahara be reached by 2024?

'Absolutely,' states the national chairperson, Susan Matutuane. 'We are blessed with an abundance of land. We have the space, youth, energy and will. The Israelis in an earlier technological age made the desert bloom. Our job is easier.

'We are re-ruralising our birthright. Commune Africa is not a movement; it is a shared spirit. Although we may never meet, we are parts of the same vision: To give urbanites a more fulfilling way of life; to make land more productive; to show those who have always lived on the land, those who are giving up hope, that the problems of drought, overgrazing and disease will be overcome. With science, commitment, water and electricity, we can rediscover Eden.'

Outreach, January 2004

nine

de-engineering: the cure for sandtonitis

Electronic mayhem in Woodmead

Mr Tony Ellert has e-mailed Consumer Focus about his new Mitsufunken Interactive TV. His first problem, once he set up the six remote speakers at the correct angles and distances, was working out how to turn it on.

The sleek cabinet, available in 12 fashion colours and three shades of black, displays no switches (being touch sensitive), and the remote control hidden in the undercarriage only reveals itself after a four-figure code is entered on the invisible keypad.

If the code is entered incorrectly, the TV emits a piercing scream as well as an alarm that is bounced by satellite to the Mitsufunken World Control Centre. This state-of-the-art anti-theft device was triggered seven times by Mr Ellert, who has trouble remembering numbers, with the result that two private security firms, the flying squad and a police helicopter surrounded his Woodmead home. After Ellert explained the problem and was unhandcuffed, a security guard showed him how to override the alarm. Then everyone left and he sat down to watch his new TV.

Unfortunately, all he could see was the Teletext in Japanese. He pressed the self-correcting fault-finder bar only to have the six speakers simultaneously recite the latest stock-market prices in Hong Kong, Bombay, Frankfurt, Paris, Lima and Warsaw.

de-engineering: the cure for sandtonitis

He loaded the interactive 'how to use your Mitsufunken' CD into his multimedia computer that reacted by showing an electronically generated Elvis Presley singing Chinese marching songs with Donald Duck and Pavarotti.

The understandably upset Tony Ellert called the Mitsufunken 24 hour World Cell Line only to be greeted by a friendly robot-helper that could speak nothing but Urdu and developed a stutter after being loudly abused.

It was at this stage that Ellert threw his cellular phone through the TV screen, triggering the anti-vandalism and terrorism devices. This time his home was surrounded by the Mitsufunken swat team who sprayed Insta-Freeze through every window. Five minutes later he was carried out in a block of ice and, after being identified, was left to thaw in the front garden.

Mr Ellert then spent seven days in an exclusive de-stress centre and sought to have the bills paid for by Mitsufunken. The company has denied liability, claiming that his initial negligence in disarming the system led to all his subsequent misfortunes. Furthermore, the company billed him with a false swat call and reprogramming costs caused by Ellert screaming at the robotic operator, which caused it electronic neural distress.

Consumer Focus has approached Mitsufunken and, after numerous tele-conferences, the company agreed to drop its actions against Mr Ellert and to replace the television, pending a personal apology to the robotic operator in its native language.

Sunday Times, April 2007

Theodore Levitt says: 'There are now steam shovels for people who haven't yet learned to use spades.'

A virulent form of steam-shovel disease has spread across South Africa. It is called 'sandtonitis', and is named after the business suburb where it claims most of its victims.

Sandtonitis is contracted after an extended stay in air-conditioned offices and boardrooms. Other contagious areas are the United States, Europe and Hong Kong. Symptoms include: 'How about a new size?', 'Give them another knob to fiddle with' and 'Let's buy a battleship'.

Sandtonitis is diagnosed when a company offers 365 colours of paint in 10 different-sized tins, while 80 per cent of the customers really need six

65

colours in two sizes at a value-driven price. We build six-lane highways and shopping malls while we lack country roads and general dealers.

Sandtonitis means over-promising, over-delivering and over-pricing. The majority of South African consumers are not born with Christofle silver spoons in their mouths and a Porsche pram in the nursery. But we don't see the majority of South Africans in our offices, in the malls or by our pools. And what you don't see doesn't really exist, does it?

For years we've known about this thing called 'the black market'. After a slide-show of township life, an expert would lecture or reassure us. Everyone is the same under the skin. Then instead of black and white, we saw blobs and bands and the new, improved Living Standards Measure (LSM) marketing model. After we look at all this, we comfort ourselves with the aspiration model that says: 'Everyone wants what we want (and have), so that's what we offer.'

The aspiration model has had great success: Lexington cigarettes were aimed at the mine manager, so all the mineworkers smoked it, Michael Jackson sold Pepsi by the truck-fleet, Princess Di, even after her death, sells more papers than a century of Popes, and most of us wouldn't mind the new Mercedes sports car. If the aspiration model was not so successful, it wouldn't be so dangerous.

Marketers aim to add value, but usually succeed only in complicating things, making them less affordable and less viable. Instead of building bridges, we raise the barriers. We manufacture more car models than countries with a market twice our size. Not surprisingly, our cars are also more expensive.

We have video recorders that only a genius or a child can use. Banks require high-rent addresses, full-colour brochures and more directors than Hollywood before they loan a roadside trader R100. Housing is unaffordable to 80 per cent of our population.

Sandtonitis is a world-wide disease. A Japanese auto giant recently offered confused buyers 73 different types of steering wheels in the year they managed to incur a billion dollar loss.

To treat the problem, ask yourself these questions daily:

- Who are my customers?
- What do they really want?
- How best can I deliver?

the prime prospect detector

Who are the people you want to reach? Try this do-it-yourself research kit. Firstly, the detector asks: Is your prime prospect a 'me', an 'us' or an 'all' kind of person? The three levels form a pyramid, rising from survival to self-indulgence.

Gauge yourself and your prime prospects on the Prospect Pyramid (below). There's one thing you can bet your Guccis on: if you want to appeal to most South Africans, you and your prospects live in different sectors.

Prospect pyramid

```
          Me
      (the haves)
         Us
    (the just-haves)
         All
    (the have-nots)
```

	Me	Us	All
Quality	Extrinsic, hyper-powerfully badged	Evident for people to see and feel	Intrinsic and durable
Variety	Me-specific, almost custom-made	Enough to dinstinguish Us from All	Doesn't really matter too much
Service	Make me feel I'm your only customer	Courtesy and sincerity, please	As long as no one's rude
Convenience	My time is extremely important	Do respect our time	Will live with inconvenience for the sake of real value
Price	I'll pay extra; it makes me feel good	We'll pay more for added value	Best possible value at best possible prices

renaissance dawning

To complicate things, you can be a 'me' when it comes to clothes, an 'us' for food and an 'all' for home furnishings. People have different priorities. You can step out of a BMW wearing a torn, freebie T-shirt because the BMW is your statement. But if you cannot afford to drive a label, you are more likely to wear one.

The prime prospect detector also finds out what motivates people. This encompasses the radicals who are inspired by hope of gain and the conservatives who are driven by fear of loss.

We all live somewhere along this continuum:

Hope of gain <----------------> **Fear of loss**

In every decision we ever make, we are bound by these polarities. Whether you think of changing your job or your fruit juice, decisions are driven by your attitude to change. You don't mind upsetting the establishment when you're not part of it. It is simpler to change your brand of rice when you make a tasteless curry. It is uncomplicated to change a bank when there aren't 20 stop-orders going through every month, and it is easier to change a government when you still live in a squatter camp.

By making the 'me/us/all' a vertical axis and the 'hope of gain/fear of loss' a horizontal axis, you can chart where your prime prospects are. Then you can begin to understand their true needs.

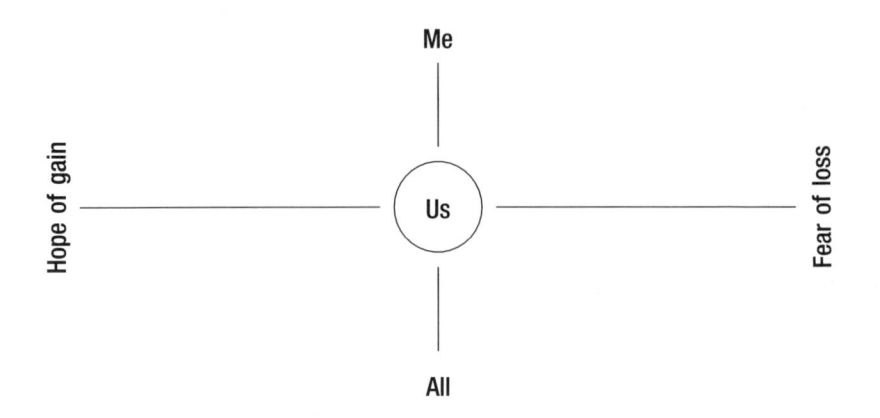

```
                    Me
                    |
                    |
Hope of gain ———————(Us)——————— Fear of loss
                    |
                    |
                    All
```

The prime prospect detector reveals the position of major players, where there is overtrading and where gaps are waiting to be filled. In

de-engineering: the cure for sandtonitis

most detectors, the gaps are found in the 'all' sector, while the 'me' and 'us' sectors are over-served.

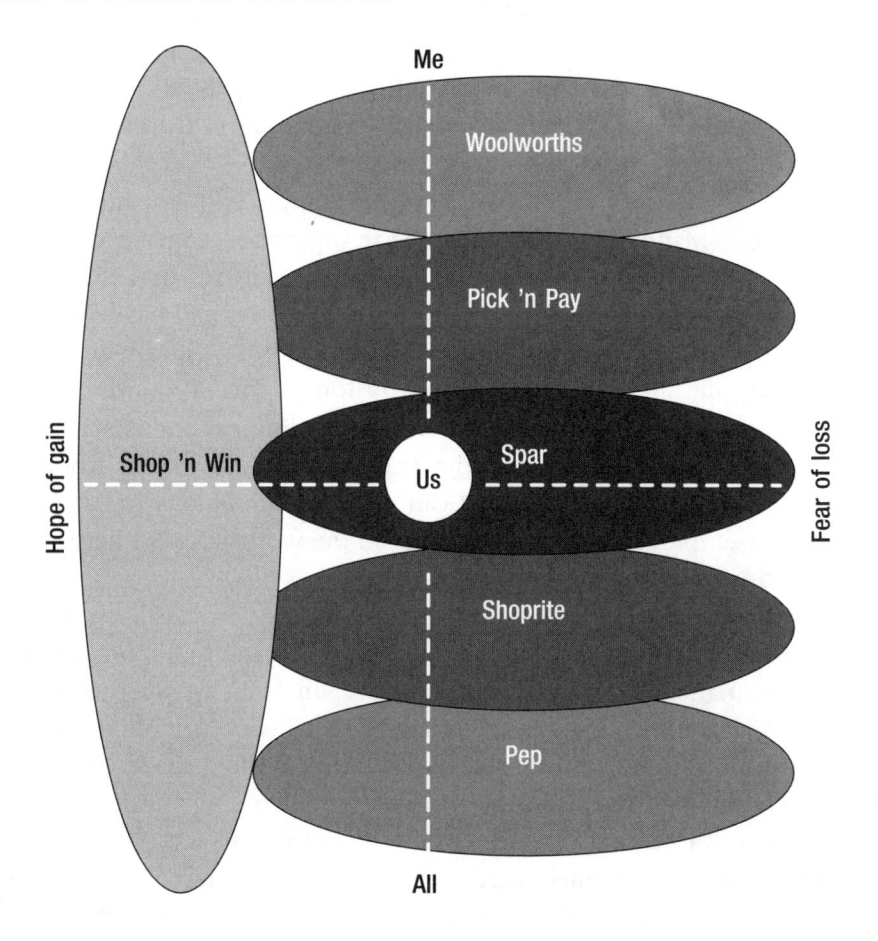

Shop 'n Win success story

The top six supermarkets of 2004 reveal a dramatic success story. Shop 'n Win, started just five years ago in containers and converted spazas, is the first to focus on the 'radical all'. By combining everyday low prices on brand leaders and own-labels with its daily lotteries, Shop 'n Win has become the fastest growing retailer of the decade.

Interestingly, customers donate about 25 per cent of their winnings to community projects, proving the supermarket's slogan: 'Everyone wins at Shop 'n Win'.

Retailing News, May 2004

renaissance dawning

the biggest spar supermarket in the world

There are more than 20 000 Spar outlets in 26 countries around the world. Where would you expect the biggest to be? In Amsterdam perhaps, as Spar started in Holland? In London, Paris, Rio or Buenos Aires? Look closer to home, but not in Johannesburg, Durban or Cape Town.

A few hours north of Durban, between Stanger and Empangeni in a town called Mandini, is the biggest Spar supermarket in the world. It started as a trading store taking up 300 square metres in 1961. Now the Rencken Spar occupies over 6 000 square metres and has 55 checkouts. Its bakery makes 12 000 loaves of bread a day, and it sells 250 tons of mealie meal and more than 100 tons of rice a month.

The statistics say 3 000 whites live in Mandini; no one is sure how many Zulus. The town is along the Tugela River, a few miles from the N2 highway. On most days you can smell the emissions from Sappi, the major employer. If the biggest Spar in the world was not here, who would dream of building one?

As you approach Rencken Spar, you pass the long wall on which schoolchildren paint scenes from their lives. The murals, sponsored by the supermarket, are changed every year. In front of the store 300 hawkers sit behind small concrete tables that Rencken built for them. They are protected from the sun by brightly coloured shade cloth that Rencken bought, and they sell most things including mealies, sweet potatoes and tomatoes, in direct opposition to their host.

Few supermarkets encourage competition, much less pay for them to compete. What is the largest supermarket in the world doing? Creating a friendly, noisy trading site that attracts everyone in the wide catchment area.

Less than a mile away is a modern, massive, under-traded OK supermarket. The corporate planners decided that whatever family Rencken could do, they could do better, and built lines of concrete stalls outside their store. Elaborate, costly structures, they are mostly empty as women traders like to sit and chat together, not stand behind counters in soulless bunkers, separated by a ton of cement.

Most Saturdays outside the Rencken Spar there is either a boxing tournament in a specially erected ring or a festival of choirs. Corporate

de-engineering: the cure for sandtonitis

planners tell you this is a really bad idea as entertainment outside stops customers going inside. Very logical, except Rencken somehow survives without corporate planners. The store managers, black and white, who all speak fluent Zulu, know the customers and their ways.

Inside the Rencken Spar, before you reach the check-out tills, there is an extra-wide walkway that stretches the length of the store. Here the community of Mandini parades and meets. On a Saturday morning while the crowd outside shout for their heroes, the walkway inside is more active than Rio de Janeiro in the rush hour.

At the Mandini OK, world-standard computer tills are silent. Managers who are experts in merchandising and human resources falter when they conduct business in Zulu. Sometimes, when they have a staff problem they ask a Rencken manager to sort it out.

At one of the Spar check-outs, a woman bent with age cashes a cheque. She has shopped here for years and the cheque is from her son, whom the manager knows. She could go to the bank, but she trusts Rencken more. And the manager trusts her.

How could you improve the biggest Spar in the world? How about a delicatessen? Even most small supermarkets have one of those; but not many in the north of KwaZulu-Natal demand Parma ham and gorgonzola.

Ask members of the Rencken family. You will find one or more of them amongst the customers, or behind the inquiry counter. Or upstairs in a small office where, hanging on the wall, is a framed black and white photograph of the original Rencken trading store. The biggest supermarket in the world is being fed by its roots.

It's the perfect antidote to sandtonitis.

our 10 areas of focus

De-engineering needs focus, and while most marketers nod religiously, saying 'we believe in focus', few accept the flip side of the coin. The chief executive officer of a retail group presented to his board 'Our 10 areas of focus'. Within a year, half of them had fallen way and the others had been diluted.

The flip side of focus is sacrifice, and that is the essence of de-engineering. What are you and, more importantly, what are your customers willing to give up? David Ogilvy, of the advertising company bearing his name, would ask prospective clients to write the essence of their company on the back of his business card.

As attention spans shorten, American marketing gurus Ries and Trout challenge you to describe your brand or company in a word; two to three if it's absolutely necessary. It's an interesting exercise, especially if six directors come up with six different words and your workforce picks six thousand more.

Sacrifice means deciding to be a low-cost dairy producer by concentrating exclusively on South Africa's three most popular flavours of yoghurt in family-size packs, two types of cheese and one kind of milk. No double-skimmed, half-skimmed fads or slow sellers. The mission is to offer South Africans the freshest, most popular dairy products at the lowest cost. Focus on value and sacrifice choice.

There are globally successful companies, such as 3M, that combine focus with diversity. They have thousands of products and they are committed to continual innovation. Their focus is their core competency. Whether it's the glue on a Post-It note or an image on film, 3M are the world experts at bonding things.

Honda can develop from lawnmowers to Formula One because its focus and strength is engine excellence. Microsoft can help you budget, manage a project, write a report and shop on a computer because it focuses on software. The day you see a Microsoft computer or dishwasher, sell the shares.

Focus and sacrifice mean you also make horrible mistakes. In early twentieth-century America, as Theodore Levitt pointed out, the railway companies concentrated on railways instead of transport. The trick is to focus on what the customer wants to buy rather than on what you want to sell.

de-engineering the country

'You are our millionth customer and we have come to your home to give you your prize. Please accept, with our compliments, a week in Mauritius.'

'Thank you.'

'Aren't you excited? Tell the camera and reporters what you're thinking right now.'

'Well, what I really want is a door for my shack.'

We need incremental housing and technologies. Site and service schemes will help more of the homeless than will dreams of three-bedroom luxury. Trading stores throughout rural areas and better local roads will do far more for southern Africa than another shopping mall or highway.

As 400 000 more homes a year spring up, so the need grows for reliable, low-cost appliances. Before we build more floodlit football and rugby stadiums, we should ensure that every township has at least one football pitch. And couldn't swimming-pools in townships take precedence over adventures on the high seas?

Tourism can mean the Lost City and Londolozi for the overseas visitor, but we need to look after our own holiday-makers as well. For the youth we should offer the Africa bus-card that can eventually take young adventurers from Cape Town to Cairo on a haphazard network of local buses. It is the best way to meet the locals and have a unique pot-pourri of experiences.

Where would our travellers sleep? They would carry home-from-home guides in their rucksacks and an African low-cost accommodation register that would advise them, if all else fails, of the nearest monastery in the Sahara that has a dormitory for praying guests.

Families that cannot afford hotels could enjoy holidays in converted army camps, with entertainment laid on 16 hours a day. If you can't have luxury, have fun.

meet the post-materialist

Growing in spending power and influence around the more prestigious suburbs of the first-world universe is the post-materialist.

The supermarket post-materialist may still have the BMW parked outside, but now it can be justified by saving on trolley-loads of own-label groceries. She knows the supermarket chain is her quality controller. Her mission is value; she enjoys, but is not fooled by, clever ads and fancy packaging. In England she buys Sainsbury and Tesco own-labels. In Germany she shops in grocery warehouses.

The fashion post-materialist in America can mix Donna Karan and K-Mart, as well as a silk scarf from Hermes with a T-shirt from the bargain bin. In South Africa, Mr Price goes with Caterpillars. The auto post-materialist has made the 4x4 the ultimate anti-urban urban statement, and the home post-materialist converts the empty kid's bedroom into a sewing-room or a book-lined study.

So what does the post-materialist want? As the body ages, the desire for health and the search for meaning re-intensifies.

Already, conspicuous consumption is being replaced by conspicuous moderation. Designer water is more fashionable than vodkatinis at power lunches. Exercise bicycles and fitness videos are the most discerning bedroom accessories. Does this mean that de-engineering will become a reverse symbol of wealth and good taste, like the chief executives who do without the corporate jet, because 'when we can afford it, we don't need it'?

> De-engineering as the cure for sandtonitis? My dear, you have it totally wrong. De-engineering is the new strain of sandtonitis. But since everyone is catching the wretched disease, why worry?

ten
the bigger picture

Ex-convicts guard world's billionaires

If you were one of the World's top 100 billionaires meeting in Davos next week, would you choose a bunch of ex-convicts to guard you? Absolutely, if they are Gamekeepers.

Founded eight years ago by two convicted felons from Soweto and a South African bank, Gamekeepers is now franchised in 30 countries, including the United States, Russia and Switzerland. Its rapid growth began in the inner cities of South Africa with businesses plagued by lawlessness turning to the new company out of desperation. And the crime rate started to fall dramatically.

There were complaints that Gamekeepers fought fire with fire. One shootout in central Johannesburg with two armed gangs left 12 dead. Since then, however, things have quietened down; grateful business people, shoppers and residents are enjoying the freedom of South African inner city streets again.

There is more to Gamekeepers success than brute force. 'We know how the mind of a thief works' says Moses Sithole, who served 15 years for a series of armed robberies. 'We know the old cons, because we were in the same places. And we are good at spotting the young ones. We can stop stuff before it gets started.'

Gamekeepers themselves remain remarkably untouched by rogue members who plague other security companies. 'We keep each other legal' Sithole says, 'we know the other side too well.'

> The motto of Gamekeepers 'Set an ex-thief to catch a thief' now has the ultimate endorsement — the 100 richest men and women in the world.
>
> Africa Bizworld, March 2010

As South Africa begins to recover her national pride and explore her diversity, the world has gone global. In this new game of universal chess, markets not countries are the pawns, castles, queens and kings.

Strategies for corporate brands such as Coca-Cola, Ford and Sony are global, and their communications are following the same route. The kind of people who buy Toyotas in Japan, America, South Africa and India have much in common. From Mamelodi to Manchester, women give Omo similar values.

While we celebrate national differences, marketers are banking billions on global similarities. Research for a washing machine may say that the Germans, Italians, French and British want different sizes, front and top-loaders, white and colour co-ordinated cabinets, but to satisfy everyone there would be dozens of models, a multiplicity of plants and high prices. What people really need are clean clothes, with the minimum of fuss, at a good price. Regional differences create niche products, while multicultural similarities create market leaders.

Service organisations are now globalising as rapidly as cars and washing powders did decades ago. Credit cards, hire cars, hotels and banks reach for the dream — one world, one brand.

what's the worth of our regional niche?

There are 175 American companies in the Fortune Global 500, and 112 from Japan. Next in line are the Europeans, with Germany having 42 companies, France 39, and Britain 35 (plus two top 50 placings belonging to a British/Dutch alliance). South Korea, despite its troubles, has 12, Australia seven, Brazil five, China four, Russia and India one apiece. Africa has none.

Excluding South Africa, the rest of the sub-Saharan region has the gross domestic product of Belgium. This means that Africa is a huge opportunity ... maybe. Multinationals are hedging their bets. The big money is being spent, and will be earned, elsewhere.

the bigger picture

Southern African companies are looking at a combination of two growth strategies. One: become stronger in local markets by making global alliances. Two: use a strong local base to enter global markets.

Banks, supermarkets, fashion stores and fast food operations developed strong distribution networks while apartheid kept many multinationals away. But as Big Mac enters the arena, Steers or Spur will eventually succumb. If Gap bring their retail formula of low-cost, fashion essentials with good service to this country, a local chain will fall by the wayside. In the global arena, distribution is a means to an end; a tactic, not a strategy. The bottom line is that a Sony is a Sony is a Sony.

Forward-looking South African companies made their global alliances a decade or more ago. Many global marriages are being arranged right now, and soon most South Africans not already in bed with a global partner will feel left on the shelf. Some will succumb to faded Casanovas on a last twirl, or young Valentinos trying their luck.

No South African corporation or brand is impregnable. It will take deep pockets for outsiders to overtake Pick 'n Pay, Edgars, Snowflake, Castle, Sanlam or Old Mutual – although it's not impossible. Imagine Tesco (placed 110th in the *Fortune* Global 500) making an alliance with Checkers; or Nippon Life (at number 19) teaming up with Momentum; or Wal-Mart (placed eighth) going into the townships. (Sam Walton became the richest man in America, pre-Buffet and Gates, by concentrating on the small towns of America. A similar opportunity awaits in southern Africa.) Industry leaders will need to be stronger than ever because there is a world of potential new alliances for the 'also-rans'. And being more powerful in local markets demands a global strategy.

There are not limitless opportunities in Africa for growth; if you want a world ranking, you need a bigger market. Mining houses, insurance companies and world-class merchant adventurers such as Anton Rupert have shown how to leverage a local stronghold to create a multinational competency. Hotel hairdriers, swimming-pool cleaners and wines are local products that made good in the world. Established and new blue chips like SAB, Gencor, Wooltru, Investec and Dimension Data pursue different paths to international acceptance. But as yet there are not many global successes rising out of Africa. And there is no global corporate brand born in Africa.

renaissance dawning

The early twenty-first century will see the war of the megabrands crossing industry barriers. Microsoft and Sony will find themselves in the same arenas, as friends or enemies. If you sell children's clothing, a major competitor is Disney; soon it could be Nintendo, or Yahoo. This doesn't mean the specialist children's shop will disappear. On the contrary, there will be a few global giants and many local independents. But those caught in the middle will suffer. Powerful local brands based on international tastes are vulnerable.

A local company can sustain a niche market by addressing local preferences, whether it's warm beer as thick as treacle in Yorkshire or samoosas to blow your head off in Durban. Frogs' legs will still sell in France, and the *fado* will always have an untranslatable Portuguese essence.

Similarly, African fashions, music and television programming are all becoming bigger business as people of all races discover African pride. Medium-sized profitable businesses that appeal to Afrocentricity will emerge. But, for African fashion to break out of its niche, it must appeal to the world. And that's done by Americanising it. Instead of flowing robes, make jeans with Ndbele trim or Zulu love letters on the pockets. Sell them in Macys and arrange for American rappers to wear them on their music videos. Africa is a strong brew; Africa Lite is far easier to swallow.

blame it all on hollywood

Charlie Chaplin, Clark Gable and Marilyn Monroe demonstrated how well global communication works. Before Hollywood, countries were separated by culture and language. James Dean, Liz Taylor and John Wayne were followed by *I love Lucy*, Bruce Springsteen and Madonna. Twentieth-century ideals of beauty and impressions of the good life have been formed in the image of America. Their cars, soft drinks and attitudes are the icons of our age. We laugh at American jokes, dream their dreams, hiss at their villains, cheer their heroes and fall in love with their stars. With jumbos and personal computers, America has made the Americanisation of the globe an interactive process. Travel and communication broaden the mind into a 12-lane highway that obeys the US rules of the road.

the bigger picture

Fortune, Time, Newsweek and *Reader's Digest* appeal to global market segments. The world watches CNN, Larry King, *Baywatch, Emergency 911* and international sport. Music videos may have local presenters and some local content, but their universal audience will be brainwashed by American fashions, American objects of desire, American angst, language and beliefs.

As America itself is a big mixing bowl of nationalities, the Americanisation of the globe is more palatable than, for instance, Japanisation. The problem is that the result can be as bland as a chain-store burger. Courtroom, hospital and police TV dramas limp along predictable plotlines. Cars, banks and department stores are researched and reproduced into unremarkable clones.

The American world needs multinational flavours.

British Airways has transformed itself from a loss-making national carrier with a disastrous reputation to 'the world's favourite airline' (that's their mission and it is near being achieved: international business travellers recently rated it second only to Singapore Airlines). It is also the world's most profitable airline. Its globalism extends from a strategy of multinational alliances to making a five million dollar commercial that is aired in over 100 countries. The commercial is Hollywood in scope; the trans-Atlantic plane you fly is American, as is the major in-flight entertainment; the wine and the duty-free perfumes are likely to be French; yet there is a tang of the British about the experience. Or rather, it is the best of British that makes the best of the world less bland. Excellent quality is expected nowadays; what also is needed is a little personality. British hospitality ranges from *Fawlty Towers* to The Ritz. British Airways are making that journey at the same time as circling the world.

You don't have to be American to profit from the Americanisation of the world. There are stories of Japanese designers from Honda who spent weeks hanging around Disneyland carparks. They were watching how American families loaded their cars. What they learnt helped them design the Civic, the first global car they produced. It became the top-selling model in the United States. Now Sony owns a major Hollywood studio. While many pundits consider Japan Inc. has taken a step too far, I wonder whether Sony is doing the ultimate America watching. Hollywood is still the dream factory of the Western world; if you can manufacture dreams, what can't you do? In animation, Disney may still reign. But a Japanese electronic games hedgehog with an attitude is more popular than Mickey Mouse amongst American boys.

Global pop culture has been Americanised, but that does not mean Americans have to control it. (After all, Hollywood was created by a small group of mid-European immigrants.) First prize is an idea that changes the world.

levi strauss and bill gates

Levi Strauss had a good idea. He turned tent cloth into trousers. It was what the market wanted. Bill Gates had a good idea too. His operating systems turned a computer into a personal computer. Many others have made jeans and computer architecture, some perhaps of better quality or better value. It's irrelevant: Levis and Microsoft are first in the global marketplace because they are first in the global mind.

Levi Strauss, the first clothing manufacturer to exceed annual sales of $5 billion, is a global mark of youth. The sense of independence, the blend of rebellion and idealism are captured in all brand communication, including the corporate management style. The company states: 'Our greatest assets are the aspirations of all those who work for us', and stringent ethical codes apply to all suppliers. This philosophy makes Levis well-made, physically and morally, in the minds of universal youth. When the philosophy is tested, the world watches.

A major Levis supplier in the East was using child labour. The automatic reaction would be: turn a blind eye or take your business elsewhere. But in that country child labour was normal, and if the supplier were fired, the hundreds of children out of work would result in suffering for many families. Levi Strauss kept on using the child-labour factory, on condition that the children spent half their time at school in a project Levi Strauss and the factory owners jointly funded. A local problem was solved in a globally acceptable way.

Today, the Levis brand is not wearing too well. The company has been missing trends and delivery dates. Being socially correct is no substitute for product and logistical excellence.

Microsoft promises faster business success, and its founder is the living personification of that dream. He is one of the two richest men in America. The other, Warren Buffet, is his friend and mentor. The global message is 'stick close to success – it rubs off'.

Apple created a superior product and more impactful advertising, but still surrendered the high ground. Microsoft is accused of unfair trade practices, withholding codes and promoting 'vapourware'. The company doesn't have the ethical high ground of Levis and it doesn't matter much. All business successes have sailed a little close to the wind. Bill Gates is the geek who took on the buttoned-down world and won; that's what matters.

If you wear Levis you're cool; if you use Microsoft you are hot property. Archetypes have always been simple; that's why they work so well. Of course, you can quite easily be using Microsoft in Levis, making you hot while you're cool. It is not the complexity of the world market that is the biggest marketing challenge, it is the complexity of a single human being.

In South Africa we have no brand archetypes with universal relevance. Even SAB, one of the world's biggest brewers, does not own a single premium brand of beer with international appeal. We have no Budweiser, Heineken or Fosters; no Sony or Samsung; no Ford, Toyota or Hyundai; no Chanel or Armani.

global leaders and followers

The great and infamous leaders in history capture their philosophies in simple, memorable thoughts: 'Only one God' ... 'Love thy neighbour as thyself' ... 'Liberté! Fraternité! Égalité!' ... 'Aryan supremacy' ... 'Think not what your country can do for you; think what you can do for your country' ... 'Total Quality Management' ... 'Re-engineering' ...

Business is the new religion of the global middle-class, complete with visionaries, leaders and false gods. Millions have worshipped at the altars of Iacocca, Trump and Buffet, read Peters and Senge more often than the Bible, and believe it's right that the chief executive of Disney is paid 10 times as much as the president of America. The deep-rooted changes that information technology and global communications are causing, together with the mystery of a new millennium, increase our need for prophets and prophecies.

The new global influencers are the management consultants and coaches that put success in a catch-phrase. Some have deep insights; some have interesting techniques; many thrive as repackagers; and a few exist on the lunatic fringe. Often, corporations lurch from one panacea to the next, while their confused employees receive another T-shirt and think if it is Tuesday, they must be re-engineering the seven habits of total quality learning organisations.

We change paradigms faster than our cars, and there is even a new business mantra intoning: 'process before content ... process before content ... process before content ...' It must keep a lot of people very busy.

Is this an age of many changes, or are we going though one huge tectonic shift? We await leaders to show us the way as our ancestors did, crouching in their caves. These leaders, if we are fortunate, will heed wise council, sense the mood of their community and see the path ahead. They will communicate a global vision to a global constituency. Our new leaders will preach a blend of worldly and other-worldly success. In the new paradigm, we can have it all.

Two thousand years ago we followed leaders with religious insights. In the last thousand years our leaders have given us nationalist dreams. And now, as we enter the next millennium, our new gurus, swapping mountain tops for laptops, show us how to run our businesses and lives in harmony. *The Seven Spiritual Laws of Success* by Deepak Chopra takes wisdoms from the Upanishads and applies them to worldly success. Charles Handy has combined careers as a religious broadcaster and business strategist. Stephen Covey, in *The Seven Habits of Highly Effective People*, threads morality with efficiency. His teachings and the Covey Leadership Centre have been likened to a messianic crusade; people come away with more than a logical, how-to-succeed-in-business kit. They return to the world as believers with a new mission in life. Our new age business leaders have turned 'greed is good' on its head. They stress an unselfish way of achieving business success, and of becoming a better and richer person.

'*Good values are good business.*' MEL ZIEGLER, founder of the Banana Republic

the bigger picture

world quality ... now with african soul

Imagine a Motorola coming out of Africa with Motorola's usual unrelenting attention to quality and innovation – but now with additional African soul. Or contemplate an African Sony with soul, a Phillips, a Toyota and a Ford with soul.

Ubuntu is part of African culture. We can ignore it; who cared about ubuntu for the last few hundred years anyway. We can use it to try to make the workers happier with their lot; who cares if the owner earns 100 times more than you; you have ubuntu, so shut up! Or we can try to make it a part of your existence and find out how can we create an ubuntu corporation that becomes a world-wide success.

Quality with African soul implies win-win situations rather than win-lose; instead of dog-eat-dog, the pack learns to live together. Ubuntu marketing, if it is from the heart, can provide a unique and relevant brand advantage in this age of bland excellence and global communication. Instead of what we can get from the consumer, ubuntu marketing asks what can we do to help our consumers help each other. How can we uplift people and bring a community closer together?

Can a brand, through actions taken in its name, become an icon of caring and a symbol of a better society?

The brand first has to deliver the formidable basics of excellent quality and value. It must tap into the universal American psyche. Americanised excellence with an ubuntu flavour could place South African brands on the world stage and even become the next business mantra. It could be a fad, or a sparkle in an idealist's eye. If ubuntu is not southern Africa's special ingredient, what is?

the universal test market

There is an opportunity to make South Africa a test market for new global technologies and brands. We are simultaneously in the agricultural, industrial and information ages. An interesting mix of communication skills is needed to reach a global banker and a traditional tribeswoman. Our phones work, airlines usually run on time, English is an official language and advertising approaches world-class standards.

Smart cards destined for America and Europe have been tried out in Alberton. If the concept fails here, not too much damage is done; the multinationals learn from their mistakes and move on to Peru or Minnesota.

Conversely, if an idea succeeds here it has a good chance of doing so in China, India, Eastern Europe and South America. A solar-powered car, houses you can build in a day, electronic learning initiatives, new financial products, and de-engineered cell phones can all have their first airing in South Africa, taking advantage of, as the South African tourism ads used to say, 'a world in one country'.

Our necessity can be the mother of world-wide invention. To steer successfully through the waters of the next decade, South Africans will have to develop great people skills. We must manage diversity, the nourishment of talent, and the aspirations of a previously repressed majority. And the skills we learn will become the core competencies of tomorrow's global service industries. What is tested here can become a benchmark for everywhere else.

trade routes

Dimension Data expands in the East, SAB in Eastern Europe, Wooltru takes over a retailer in Australia and Investec builds up its presence in Britain. Companies ranging from Engen to Protea Stores and the Conservation Corporation are building a pan-African network. Giants of the Johannesburg Stock Exchange know they must internationalise, even as they defend their home turf from foreign invaders.

Few have taken the American route, citing the high cost of entry. But perhaps we want too much too quickly. In 1960, with a capital investment of $500 000 Sony set up shop in the United States in a small New York City warehouse, employing six people. Today, Sony Electronics in North America represents the largest single geographical operation of the Sony Corporation, with almost $10 billion sales and 24 000 employees. Consumers have voted Sony the number one brand in America, ahead of Coca-Cola and McDonald's. It is also one of the top 10 United States patent holders. Sony had a mission – to prove to the world that the Japanese can make superior quality electronic products – and started at a time when anything from the land of the rising sun, whether a car or a battery, was dismissed as 'Jap crap'. Today, in a world that never even considers anything African to be of international value, is the time for an African Sony to show the way. It may take more than 30 years – all the more reason to start now.

While the South African giants (and their stakeholders) take their first tentative steps onto the world stage, the entrepreneurs of tomorrow still linger in the wings.

Eighty per cent of all small and medium enterprises (SMEs) in Italy are exporters; 37% in the United States, 20% in the UK and 14% in Canada. The contribution to total exports by SMEs range from Taiwan – 56%, and Italy – 53%, to Canada – 9%.

By contrast, less than 3% of all South African SMEs are exporters, accounting for less than 1% of export sales. Whilst Anglo American, Barlows or Liberty remain outside of the global top 500, indicating that South Africa has yet to join the premier league, the failure of our SMEs to make any impact on exports shows that we still do not know how to play the global game.

The bigger picture is not only for bigger players – the world is wide open for one-man shows, like the 60-year-old in a Sea Point flat who has developed an internet site billed as the world's ultimate directory of *gratis* software and now collects advertising revenues in dollars.

eleven
never rub bottoms with a porcupine

Gold-encrusted popcorn

Visit the new Saigon or the old Shanghai. Stop over in New Delhi, Nairobi, Petrograd or Patagonia and you will come across the golden peacock. He may be your tour guide, a hotel night manager, a salesman, or rising executive.

Marketers call him the aspirational male, and throughout the developing world he affirms his status with chains, bracelets and diamond rings. The flash of gold around his neck and on his wrist are his statement of arrival.

But after the chain and bracelet, what's next? Gold Africa think they have the answer. The peacock is being offered 24-carat trouser nuggets. Living in your trouser pocket, they are meant to be felt rather than seen. Each is individually created in the heat of African furnaces, overseen by an African nugget-crafter trained in Italy.

The 'Is it art, craft or obscenity?' row erupted after their launch. International supermodels talked lovingly about a man's 'pure 24' trouser-pocket nuggets. 'Twentieth-century sexists!' shouted the multinational women's libbers in the 'Squash their nuggets' protest.

'Hands off our nuggets' advertisements then appeared with this message: 'Gold, hidden for millions of years underground, has learnt to glow secretly, and that is what it does in your pocket, giving you hidden power in the office, self-confidence on the golf-course and allowing you to be the centre of attraction amongst friends.

'When doubt assails you, slip a hand into your trouser-pocket and play with your nugget. Roll it around surreptitiously, squeeze the cool protuberances and be reassured that your life is not totally without success.'

The African heritage adds global converts who say there is powerful goodness in trouser nuggets. They ward off bad luck, a faithless partner, tiredness and angst. Their critics dismiss the nuggets as 'gold-encrusted popcorn' and a crude attempt to make the peacock buy more ore.

These critics, in turn, are dismissed as 'limp-wristed filigrees' by millions of golden peacocks who celebrate success in their trouser pockets.

African Trade, May 2009

South Africa has always undersold its natural assets, perhaps because it has so many: gold, diamonds, natural beauty, animals, sun, space and big horizons. Others from continents less blessed with natural assets saw the value of ours. They are closer to the markets and understand them better. Like the diamond-cutters of Amsterdam and the gold-designers of Italy, they create industries far removed from the source.

An abundance of natural assets is an obvious combination of blessing and curse. It invites colonialisation. It encourages huge divisions between a few haves and many have-nots. In this environment, the work ethic is easily lost.

The middle class is the heart of democracy, yet until recently it has hardly existed in Africa. The middle class was suppressed for generations by the economics and politics of exclusivity and fear.

Meanwhile, the world demands our raw materials and we trade away Africa's birthright. We grow the trees and spend billions turning wood into world-quality paper. We sell it to the East. Then they print the books that we buy back for many times the price we were paid.

Why do we grow the trees and make the paper for Britain and Singapore to print? Why do we mine gold with which Italy and India design? Italy's gold industry is bigger than ours. With our capital and labour we take the lion's share of the risks, then squander the lion's share of the rewards.

Two of South Africa's beneficiated industries worthy of pride are wine and steel. But something is amiss if we can earn more from a grape than from a tree. Our natural resources have made South Africa a world business. Beneficiating them will make the business a success.

the cluster of gold

The average gold price in 1995 was $384, by 1998 it tumbled to $270. Meanwhile South Africa's gold production slips and labour costs rise. Mining houses have only the collapsing rand and downsizing to thank for their profits.

But South Africa cannot turn away from gold; we must maximise the opportunity, not the problem.

If South Africa begins to market itself effectively, we will focus on three to five key business clusters in which we can have a sustainable global competitive advantage. In the past we tried to promote a laundry list of 20-plus industries. It makes sense that one cluster is gold.

The many uses of gold – as adornment, currency, a functional metal and investment – provides for a wide spectrum of business opportunities.

Mining houses will change their nature. We can expect some of the mega-mergers that are changing the oil industry to be mirrored in gold. For instance, if Anglogold (number one gold producer in the world) ties the knot with Barrick (based in the USA and the world's number two) the resulting mining giant would have gold operations spreading across the five continents. Mega-mergers could also lead to higher valuations for South African mines, facilitating the finance of projects, that in turn stimulate the economy. Smaller mining houses are likely to be trampled underfoot as the giants dance.

South African gold mines that do not take the global plunge will need to find other sources of revenue. Either they move downstream into businesses like refining and design, or they could be acquired by a brand-orientated luxury-goods company that treats the gold mine as just another form of manufacturing plant.

Other mines will divest themselves of their underlying assets and then market their human resources, becoming specialised gold mining consultancies. They will offer project management, research and development, producing new technologies that make Africa, once again, the global home of gold.

never rub bottoms with a porcupine

The Akan people of Ghana and the Ivory Coast have traded in gold for over 500 years; their territory still contains rich alluvial gold-fields. Akan leaders formed the Asante State at the turn of the 18th century. It grew through military conquest and wealth, its culture filled with a lavish use of gold and gold-plated adornments.

A series of gold-weights were created, representing animals and proverbs. One is a headless fish. It symbolises the story of a chief who catches a fish then presents the head to his first and older wife. He gives the edible part to his younger and favourite wife. The older woman kills herself with grief over the insult, and the chief instructs his goldsmith to make the headless fish to remind him of the discord that is the result of an unjust action.

The gold peanut recalls the Akan proverb, 'Marriage is like groundnuts: you have to crack them open to see what's inside'. The porcupine is the Asante national emblem. Its quills are the Asante warriors and the porcupine gold-weight is rich in symbolism. One proverb it recalls is: 'Never rub bottoms with a porcupine'. In other words, don't get involved in a dispute with someone stronger than yourself.

The Asante forgot this proverb as they grew to threaten the European gold and slave interests. An escalating series of conflicts with the British, who had become the major European power along the West African coast, led to the Asante defeat in 1900 and its inclusion in the Gold Coast. At the same time, the gold trade and the art of Akan goldsmiths went into decline.

Women in Ghana today continue to pan for gold. Men dig pits in the sediment, and after a heavy rain you see village children go out with their pans to find gold traces in the earth-compacted streets. Ghana exports over $200 million worth of gold a year, almost a quarter of its foreign exchange earnings. Very little is beneficiated; the art of the Asante empire has been consigned to British museums and American collectors.

From the time of the Pharaohs, gold has been crafted in Africa. 'When a shield wears out,' another proverb tells us, 'the framework still remains.'

from the mandela to gold-eating plants

South African gold-mines are the most marginal in the world, surviving between the flashpoints of low productivity and low-cost labour. The good news is that the world consumption of gold is increasing. This rise is driven by users, not governments and speculators. Less than 20 per cent of annual sales remain as gold bars. So, encourage users and you have a long-term recipe for a better gold price.

Yet if gold chains and bracelets become a fad, a part of mafia culture, or over-materialist, the growing gold boom could fail. Gold has noble credentials and it is time they were re-presented.

Three years ago, in the first edition of this book, I suggested that the largely discredited Krugerrand should make way for 'the Mandela'. Researching this edition, I am told that the Mandela was considered, but it is likely the Krugerrand will receive more positive government support. I also suggested that 'the profits could go to the Mandela Trust, a foundation dedicated to skills training. We can create the Gauteng Gold College that will teach design and seed an industry'. We shall see.

We will also see a profusion of new products and services. Twenty-four carat hard gold, made by innovative technologists, will become a high-ticket fashion statement as the finest work is done on the purest gold. Mini gold bars with unique holograms (for security and show), segmented gold bars (so the patriarch can share his wealth with his children and his children's children), and scented gold (that's aromatherapeutic) are some of the possibilities being tested. Although there are no plans right now for gold trouser nuggets, anything is possible.

The biggest users of gold come from the East. These gold bugs want their metal to be purer than is possible. This means 24 carat and a new minting that guarantees the gold did not come from the teeth of a holocaust victim. Apart from the morality, the Chinese especially are superstitious. The promises of purity and virgin gold mined from the deepest mines in the world could catch these gold bugs.

Convenience is another motivator. Put the Mandelas into vending machines at the departure halls of our international airports, payable by credit card; create an Internet gold site (24caratgallery.com) that exhibits and sells the very best, delivery within 24 hours at designated South African 5 star hotels; and if the crime wave recedes introduce curb-side goldsmiths who have upgraded from wire sculptures to gold wire.

We can cater quite well for the tourist trade, but what about the locals? A gold culture in this country can be created as soon as the laws are changed to allow South Africans to own investment gold. There will be savings schemes, like the Gold Accumulation Plan from India, that encourages the non-wealthy to build up a store of gold. Banks will display and sell gold and there has even been talk of a new pan-African gold standard – a common currency that is backed, at least in part, by the precious metal.

Gold can even beautify the South African environment. There are certain plants that naturally absorb gold. Seed them on all the mine dumps surrounding Johannesburg and the parched, dusty mounds will be transformed into lush, green hills. And an industry, the gold harvest, will be born: a new tourist attraction for *Egoli* – place of gold.

branding african gold

Titan of India, the world's biggest watch company, now manufactures jewellery designed in the European capitals of taste and fashion. South Africa can take a gold leaf out of their book.

We need to tempt leading Italian gold designers to come to Gauteng. Mining houses can enter into joint ventures with manufacturers in India. The greatest gold artists and craftsmen in the world will be our teachers. Trainees with the most promise can be apprenticed to their studios and factories. We need to be commercially enlightened, learning the secrets of style, quality and mass production.

Along the way we may rediscover African secrets and traditions. Zimbabwe had gold-mines before the birth of Christ. Its gold was

renaissance dawning

traded over a thousand years ago for oxen and salt. Modern beneficiation could lead to an African renaissance. African gold from Ghana, Tanzania, Zimbabwe and South Africa will combine modern taste with tradition. Gold bracelets with porcupines and peanuts mean more than horseshoes and four-leaf clovers.

As our manufacturing and design ability improve, and as we become more in touch with our market and our roots, we will create a demand for an African gold brand. A co-ordinated marketing strategy should increase demand each year ahead of supply. For Africa to grow stronger, mealie meal must be more available and gold more in demand.

The African goldmark on jewellery will provide added emotional value. Excellent style and quality are the minimum stakes in the new world game. Once Africa achieves this, we have the edge. We are where the gold comes from. Canadian and Australian gold do not have the sound of added value. The Chinese have jade, of course, but not gold. Russian and African gold are the two players with spiritual gravitas. And of the two, African gold has the infrastructure.

The framework of the shield still exists. Do we have the vision to re-create the covering?

Since the first edition of this book, published three years ago, an initiative has begun to brand African gold. 'Ra' is a premium brand that uses only best quality gold, combined with technological innovation, consistent quality and design flair. (I am a consultant to the project, and therefore I am enthusiastic.)

Ra by Dior

This month, all American Express Platinum cardholders will receive their Ra by Dior multimedia catalogue. It is a cornucopia of beauty. Long necks, slim wrists, elegant fingers, ankles and ears are all enhanced by Ra gold and jewels. Click to stop the show, or relax and let sensuality surround you.

Close-up images of beautiful gold-jewelled people merge into styles and prices. It is a journey of the senses from the oldest continent on earth, through timeless beauty, to the look of today and tomorrow. Ra is gold and Dior is style. Their global marriage provides ravishing opportunities for on-line purchasing.

Advertorial from Fortune, May 2009

golden dreams

I asked Sarah da Vanzo, managing director of Consolidated Bullion, the creator of Ra and source of many of these gold musings, for other undreamed-of possibilities. Here are some ideas:

> **MotherNatureGold** *Gold that has been mined, not by man, but Mother Nature. Gold is found in African flora and fauna, as well as on the back of a particular spider. This natural gold will command a huge premium.*
>
> **GreenGold** *Green-tinted gold made from recycled mine dump material and sold through the World Wildlife Fund.*
>
> **SmartGold** *Gold bars embedded with smart card micro-chips will have proof of ownership as well as a guaranteed minimum buy-back price.*
>
> **NewAgeGold** *Your 24 carat gold tuning fork will resonate at the meditational frequency of your choice; and your set of gold nose-rings are embedded with a selection of scents to stimulate different moods.*
>
> **HealthGold** *There is a body of evidence suggesting that a band of gold is better for arthritis than a band of copper. Chinese and Indians eat and drink flecks of gold for their health. Can South Africa pioneer Gold Spas, the ultimate re-energising experience for the wealthy age-averse? Pure spa baths flecked with gold, the laying on of gold and fruit plants being fed gold solutions, yielding crops of gold-laced fruit.*

south african trees; made in singapore

The apartheid years created Fortress South Africa that, amongst other things, protected and isolated local industries. World quality and productivity revolutions swept by us, hardly noticed.

Now we fall further behind as pent-up wage demands, the national employment drive and unrealistic expectations make us even less competitive. Global industry demands efficiency with a remorselessness that is deflected only by gross moral injustice. In most cases, we fall woefully short on quality, price and reliable delivery dates.

We have an unemployment rate of over 40 per cent. In Singapore there is no such statistic. Yet it pays South African publishers to export the words, pictures and paper for printing and eventual re-importation. We are poor farmers selling fresh oranges to buy orange juice.

There are excellent printers and publishers throughout South Africa. During the isolation years, we won hundreds of international awards for books, annual reports and print advertisements. The commercial world was hostile to us, and so we competed more for glory than business, and more as individuals than as South Africans. We have proven we are world class, now we must marry quality and low cost – just like the rest of the world.

Achievable targets for our printing industry include achieving 10 times the number of high-quality art books for overseas markets than we do now, producing inter-regional editions for global magazines, printing CD covers and telephone directories for Africa and the Middle East.

The industry needs high-productivity printing methods and machines that could be partly financed by local paper-mills. Through a unified vision and effort, a South African tree may finally be as valuable as a South African grape.

follow the wood

In Malawi you will find wood carvings at most road intersections and in every market. The majority are made at high speed in village factories for the casual tourist. If you scratch the base of some, you will find that the ebony is really mahogany covered in black shoe polish. If you want the genuine article, you must find the artists who follow the wood. A sculptor finds a good ebony tree and moves there to live and work. His family goes with him. They are craft-nomads, living next to their source of livelihood and inspiration.

The forests of South Africa can spawn their own communities of crafts people. For mass rural production, consider an export business in wooden garden furniture. White plastic is ecologically and garden-unfriendly, especially when compared to the natural qualities of sealed, unpainted wood.

Plastic is cheap and certainly not the real thing. South Africa can pledge itself to plant more trees than it uses, and a CNN World Report will show global villagers how their choice of garden furniture lifts rural communities out of the poverty trap. The pleasure derived from this, however, is only the icing; the whole cake has to be delicious.

The wooden garden furniture industry in South Africa began as a side-of-the-road affair. Designs are basic, while marketing and guarantees are almost non-existent. Despite this, the industry thrives because a need is being met. The consumer is talking to us.

Malaysia has a strong export business in wooden garden furniture. They have wonderful wooden swing seats and elegantly carved loungers. Again, we can learn from the best, engaging the traditional skills of carvers from Malawi, Mozambique and Zimbabwe, while marketers in South Africa remind the world how tired everyone is of plastic living. If the price is reasonable, and the product looks good, feels good and helps the under-privileged while also being ecologically correct, it is a worthy cause – and a good conversation piece.

Offcuts of the trees also have economic value. Hand-carved masks and statues will be sought after by tourists and the new Africans who have pride in their continent as well as more space to fill in their homes.

These masks and statues need not have tribal roots. Rural twenty-first century wood sculptors will create their own legends, sculpting villages and animals, as well as politicians, drilling rigs and city life. The modern and traditional will form new global visions of Africa.

Our budding Hepplewhites, Michelangelos and Rodins will be found near the wood that becomes their inspiration and income. Around them, small craft factories will grow, creating clusters of rural excellence.

We can invite international interior designers to come over and share with us the kind of sculptures they look for; the homes, gardens and boardrooms they will grace. And while the designers enlighten the carvers, the carvers must seek to enchant the designers, sending them home with new ideas and opening up new markets.

As electricity reaches these rural areas, wood will no longer be needed for fuel. Instead of being burnt, it will be beneficiated. Rural communities will be encouraged to plant new trees, to ensure their children and children's children will continue to profit from their growing skills.

the beneficiation of people

South Africa has trees and gold, poverty and hunger. Our natural resources have made only some of us rich. Beneficiation will benefit everyone. The success of African gold will create a new generation of crafts people, join countries across Africa in a sustainable, profitable venture and keep open marginal mines. It will provide employment for tens of thousands, as well as skills upgrading and opportunities for new entrepreneurs. And it could earn Africa billions.

The beneficiation of our trees will save villages, help communities learn world-class skills and earns us hundreds of millions of dollars.

What else is there?

We need a register of all the natural assets our continent provides and ways they can be beneficiated, from solar power to cotton shirts. The Beneficiation Bank will be a commercial trans-African initiative, providing finance for programmes that make the most of what Africa offers. The bank will co-ordinate and prioritise the regional and local opportunities, unify industries across national boundaries and investigate new world markets.

But all these are dreams without the most important beneficiation process of all – the beneficiation of people. Studies around the world show that 40 to 90 per cent of a nation's economic growth relies on technological advances and knowledge growth. South Africa needs engineers and scientists.

In the United States there are over 126 000 engineers and scientists per million people; in Europe there are 50 000 per million and in South Africa the figure is 17 000 per million. Without more trained people this country is unlikely ever to become a leader in anything except mining.

South Africa under-spends drastically on research and development. The developed nations spend almost 2,8 per cent of their gross domestic product (GDP) on research and development; South Africa spends less than 0,8 per cent. It is interesting that South Korea's recent prosperity has come after a concerted effort to outspend, in percentage terms, the developed nations. By the year 2000, more than 4,5 per cent of their GDP will be devoted to research and development. (While South Korea has struggled recently, we can still learn much from a country ravaged by war in the 1950s, and with 12 companies in the *Fortune* Global 500 we enter the new millennium.)

In Japan, 80 per cent of research and development money is funded by industry; in the UK and USA it is over 70 per cent. In South Korea, the private sector contributes 60 per cent. In South Africa, industry is far more tight-fisted, providing less than 30 per cent of national research and development funding.

Business has taken a short-term view of South Africa Inc. for many years. Companies with overseas head offices have become the new colonialists. Many arrive with promises of a better life, only to carry as much gold as possible back to their court and king.

South Africa needs affirmative spending on research and development to make up for past neglect. For instance, pharmaceutical companies that do business here should be encouraged to investigate our native plants and flowers, hundreds of which are used by different tribes for their medicinal properties. Substantial research and development involving chemists, inyangas and sangomas will result in an exchange of skills and possibly a new, naturally-based wonder drug.

American computer companies have set up sales and support offices in southern Africa; the research is done back home. That's why most software is developed for American needs. If all computer companies here put five per cent of their turnover into research, we may begin to see high-tech African solutions.

Will construction companies invest in the search for low-cost building methods?

Around the world automobile companies spend over 2,5 per cent of their total sales on research and development. Locally the figure is less than 0,08 per cent. That is under one-thirtieth of a fair share. It is not surprising that no car or truck has been designed specifically for Africa.

How much do financial institutions spend on research and development? How much do IT and office equipment companies spend? Local, regional and national governments should ask this question before they award a contract. Companies can ask each other, making it an issue.

Stock-market investors would also like to know; what you spend on research and development is an indicator of your health and the nation's. If we want a success story here, we need to spend 500 per cent more than we do.

The World Bank states that Africa's success or failure rests on its ability to compete. That means we must rub bottoms with the porcupines of America, Japan, Germany and Singapore. It will be an extremely painful experience ... unless we become porcupines too.

Billions of years ago, Nature provided Africa with its quills. Beneficiation of our people will allow them to grow and sharpen their points. It is high time.

twelve
hooked on hemp

'The lethal dose of cannabis is a two-kilogram block dropped on your head from the twenty-fifth floor of a high-rise building.'

A British overview of international research findings

Growing dagga supports over 250 000 rural farmers and their families in southern Africa. While the crop remains illegal, we are committed to punishing these farmers and destroying their livelihoods, driving them from the land into an uncertain urban future. Alternatively, the country can turn a blind eye to their activities, encouraging them and others to be lawless. Banning dagga creates an untenable situation; so how about encouraging it?

Recorded uses of the hemp plant go back almost 9 000 years. The earliest known fabric was made of hemp. It clothed the soldiers of the Roman Empire. The first pair of Levis was cut from hemp cloth. The American Declaration of Independence was drafted on hemp paper. Most canvas paintings, including those by Rembrandt and Van Gogh, were on hemp canvas. ('Canvas' is Dutch for the Greek word 'cannabis'.) Queen Victoria took marijuana for her period pains and today marijuana tea is still offered as a general remedy.

Hemp is a rich source of fibre that can be used to make rope, sails, bedding for horses and paper. It can also be used to make a woven cloth with a linen texture that is more durable than cotton. It is far easier to grow than other natural fibres. It does not need the costly, ecophobic pesticides that must be used to protect plants like cotton.

Hemp has long been a vital part of rural and developing economies. It was not illegal before the twentieth century when, according to the dope legends, Du Pont pressurised the United States government into banning the evil weed in an effort to promote its new wonder fibre, nylon.

Today it is taken by sufferers of glaucoma (it helps to reduce pressure on the optic nerve), AIDS patients (to improve appetite), the spinally injured (it reduces spasms) and sufferers of chronic multiple sclerosis (to relieve pain and muscular spasm). In a South African survey, seven out of 10 doctors agree off the record that cancer patients should use dagga to reduce the severe nausea caused by their cocktail of prescribed drugs.

Should dagga be freely available? Many who disagree claim that marijuana is a path to harder drugs, and they are right. But is it a social path because our laws throws the pot smoker and the heroin addict together? The legalisers claim that if dagga is unbanned, marijuana smokers are as unlikely to snort cocaine or shoot heroin as whiskey drinkers. This is an unproven hypothesis.

It is likely that, if dagga is unbanned, more would smoke it.

Do we protect a traditional rural industry, try to squash it or pretend it doesn't exist? Is dagga an avenue to hard drugs or can it be a barrier? Do we make it freely available? Is there a way to the moral high ground, as well as the bag of gold?

And what's the worst that can happen if we do nothing?

alex on crack

When South Africa re-opened to the world, illegal as well as legal trade took off. We are targeted by multinational drug cartels as a fertile area for growth. Along with uppers, downers, cocaine, heroin and opium, we are about to experience crack. It is a low-cost, vicious, highly addictive form of cocaine. In America crack thrives on inner city hopelessness, youth and anger. The high one experiences is intense and short-lived. Addicts steal, maim and kill for one more hit and its resulting feeling of omnipotence. Crack turns communities into neighbourhoods from hell.

hooked on hemp

Main dealers form networks of user-dealers in schools and gangs. The first couple of hits are give-aways; then you must pay. While you have the money, you can afford to feed your habit. If you're an unemployed youth, you sell your body for sex or start a career of crime. Stealing money, credit cards and watches will graduate to holding up motorists, and one day, in a crack rage, shooting a woman for her bag of groceries.

Meanwhile the drug gangs fight for turf and bloody wars erupt. The violence escalates and everyone in the community becomes a drug victim.

In Washington DC, less than a mile from the White House, there are violent no-go areas. Buses with armed guards have been hijacked, and children are casually machine-gunned.

That is happening in the home of the free. Now imagine crack invading South African townships. The rage already exists. So does poverty and hopelessness. Guns are more common than jobs. Already Johannesburg is the death capital of the world. The good guys are bad and the bad guys are good. Amongst the dealers will be unemployed, ex-guerilla fighters, while amongst the police are those who used to break down residents' doors at four in the morning.

In the *favelas* of Brazil, drug-lords sponsor local football teams and the police are known as child killers. In many townships, the police are still the enemy; the invader. And while invaders win battles, they rarely win wars.

The window of opportunity for the drug barons and crime syndicates is wide open. By making their overseas alliances, they seek to control the townships and inner cities.

The poor have political power and no jobs. The guns are in place. The police are under suspicion (a recent survey suggests that South African police are three times more likely to commit a crime than the average citizen). Add crack, stand back and watch for the explosion. Crack rage in Alex; crack rage in Crossroads, Umhlazi and Daveyton. The country would become ungovernable; no one will be safe.

the government on drugs

World-wide, the drug policy debate centres on the allocation of funds for detection and punishment versus funds for treatment and rehabilitation. Trying to do one job properly seems to compromise the other.

In America, funds have been diverted from treatment to detection, and massive swoops are made, yet only 10 per cent of cocaine coming into the United States is confiscated. The police are losing control of the inner cities, addicts are gun-fodder, and gangs declare war on human decency, the law and each other.

The Singapore option is to hang all the dealers. But giving the death-sentence for selling two grams of cocaine, while unrepentant killers enjoy indemnity and state pensions, is not a serious political option in South Africa.

We cannot be soft on drugs and we cannot be seen as monsters. While we prevaricate, the townships begin to self-destruct. If the battle has hardly commenced in the inner cities, it is already being lost at the long, under-manned national borders. Refugees pour in by bus, by truck and on foot, many risking the wild as they race through the Kruger Park. Some take AK47s to trade as they start a new life while others are given hard drugs to carry that are swiftly collected when they cross successfully.

If we cannot stop the supply, we have to decrease the demand. That will depress the price and make this country less lucrative for the global drug barons. The Americans tried massive TV campaigns, but consumer behaviour was hardly affected. We can learn only so much from overseas experience; we need an African solution.

Crack is a cheap escape from reality, as is dagga. Crack is an intense high; dagga has a calming effect. The effect of crack quickly dissipates, leaving a craving for more. The effect of dagga slowly fades away, and the only craving is for food. While dagga and drink cause unpredictable behaviour, the dagga smoker is a danger to society only if he is allowed to drive, to operate heavy machinery, or make a speech about the meaning of life.

Too much dagga creates listlessness and a lack of productivity. Too much crack unhinges the mind and destroys society. For the addictive personality, dagga is the lesser of the two evils. To combat crack with dagga would make the farmers happy and the townships stoned. It is not a perfect solution.

There is strong and weak dagga, prized blends like 'Malawi Cob' and

'Durban Poison', as well as the pips and twigs of garage 'zoll'. If the industry came out of the shadows, the first thing it would need would be quality control.

dagga lite

The toxicity of dagga plants is controllable. In other words, you can grow dagga that makes someone very stoned, slightly stoned or not stoned at all.

While the dagga is unregulated and illegal, you might as well go for maximum strength. If the law allowed you to continue with your business as long as you reduced the toxicity, you would consider the deal. If the new buyers of your crop were regular payers and helped you produce more, your increasing affluence would show others that low toxicity equals high profits.

The buyers would be cigarette companies allowed to sell 'Dagga Lite', containing extra-low toxicity and no nicotine. Regulations concerning Dagga Lite could be similar to alcohol: no sales to minors, being stoned at work would be a dismissable offence and driving under the influence would take you straight to jail. Better detection methods will stop many of the chancers.

> Competing for space with Peter Stuyvesant and Benson & Hedges on pub, café and supermarket shelves are Dagga Lite brands such as 'MJ Ultra Mild' and 'Swazi Smiles'.

> Is lighting up replacing drinking down? It's a hot topic at liquor producer power lunches, where the waft of 'Blue Transkeis' mixes with the aroma of Chardonnay.

> Low-toxicity farmers welcome their legal status as well as the help they receive from the Hemp Foundation. It is funded by the Dagga Lite cigarette companies with 20 per cent of their income. As well as making farmers more productive, the foundation researches and markets the eco-friendliness of hemp.

Fresh Cream, June 2004

eat, drink and be happy

Hemp seed contains all eight amino acids essential to human nutrition; it is high in calcium, magnesium, phosphorus, potassium, carotene, sulphur, iron and zinc, as well as vitamins A, E, C, B1, B2, B3, and B6.

Hemp food and beverage products include hemp oil and seed, flour, pasta, cheese, tofu, salad dressings, snacks, sweets, protein powders, soft drinks, beer, and wine. Hemp beer is produced and sold in Europe and the US.

The major use of hemp fibre in Europe is in the production of speciality papers such as cigarette paper, archival paper, tea bags, and currency paper. In the United States, hemp has been bonded with artificial fibres. Until the 1930s, hemp-based cellophane, celluloid and other products were widely-used, and Henry Ford used hemp to make car doors and fenders. Today, hemp fibres are introduced into plastics to make them stiffer, stronger and more impact resistant. Hemp plastic products include chairs, boxes, percussion instruments, lampshades, bowls, cups, spectacles, jewellery, skateboards, and snowboards.

This hemp is not the same plant as the one that produces dagga, but it is a close cousin and substitution should be relatively easy.

the height of eco-chic

To encourage farmers to grow the low and non-toxic versions of the crop, the whole plant should be sellable. At the moment, only the leaves and seeds have any economic value. If hemp clothing becomes fashionable, the whole plant will be prized. In addition, South Africa will have a new commodity to export.

South Africa would not be the first country to unban hemp for clothing. For a few years now there has been a European Community subsidy of R2 000 an acre to grow hemp. Farmers taking advantage of it have re-discovered a low-maintenance crop that yields up to three harvests a year. It grows easily – even in cold, damp England, as place-names like Hemel Hempstead testify.

Although hemp is mainly being grown for horse-bedding and paper-making, outlets such as England's The House of Hemp make T-shirts, jeans and shorts. Eco-entrepreneurs finance Thai farmers and Indian collectives, but so far it has all been fringe production, like the Ganjaland T-shirts people wear on coach tours of Amsterdam coffee houses.

In Europe, growing hemp is an experiment. In South Africa it is the way a quarter of a million people live, and if we create an export market, it could support another quarter of a million. We cannot let hemp remain on the hippy fringe. It is too eco-chic.

The product needs improvement. The fabric often has a rough texture that, while attractive to the eye, makes more sensitive skins itch. Perhaps it needs to be blended with artificial or other natural fibres; perhaps it needs to be treated or woven in a different way. The problem certainly needs some committed research. Where the itch is not so prevalent – in home furnishings – hemp is already securing its place on the fashion stage. From Kashgar carpets to Tessa Sonik's new collection of coverings, hemp is growing – but the hemp they use is imported. We imprison and destroy our cash-cows only to buy our milk and meat from halfway across the world.

Hemp needs to be positioned in the fashion buyer's mind between cotton and linen, with the added dimension of bringing variety into the wardrobe. Eco-fashion started in the 1990s as a reaction to the artificiality of the 80s. First-world women can justify the luxury of a linen suit by feeling vaguely positive about doing something for the environment. As this obscure do-goodism evaporates over the next few years, the opportunity for hemp will grow. There is nothing vague about helping a million rural poor in southern Africa and India. The clothes we wear will not be saving the boll-weevil. They will be saving people.

To make hemp mainstream, we need to raise awareness, create concern, and gain commitment amongst the small, tightly-focused group of people who can make the most difference. Hemp must move and inspire the great fashion designers of the world.

While dagga may remain the evil weed, its cousin hemp can become part of the new afro-cool. Instead of police setting fire to the harvest, agronomists and bankers will help farmers with yields and loans.

Richard Jones, an Australian MP, stood up in parliament in a suit made from Chinese hemp and suggested that cultivation of the plant would boost his country's economy. We await our own politicians' fashion show: the President sporting a hemp shirt, the Speaker resplendent in her hemp robes and sandals, and the new Nats in hemp safari suits. Or at the very least, we await to hear what we are going to do about 250 000 farmers and families who live by growing an illegal substance.

The chic of it

From the high priests of American hip-hop to the acolytes of Armani, the leaders and chief disciples of fashion were flown to remote farmlands in KwaZulu, Swaziland and the Transkei. They saw the new, safe ganja being grown and woven. They made suggestions and, more importantly, they began to care.

Within 12 months, hemp skirts, jeans, jackets and shorts were seen on music videos and fashion runways. The Dior showstopper was the Hemp Wedding, followed by trails of Dagga Lite incense. Then Levis simultaneously opened its KwaZulu and Calcutta factories, making Hemp 501s for the world. Now hemp is walking out of the stores and onto the streets, the latest cover of Vogue features a marijuana fig-leaf as the supermodel's only adornment, with the theme 'Hooked on Hemp'.

Fresh Cream, June 2004

thirteen
return of the wrigglies

Kiddie-licious mopane burgers

This winter warm them up when they race home from school: Give them easy-to-make, kiddie-licious mopane burgers!

Kids love the little worms. While some of us older folk still go cold at the thought, you can now buy a hot mopane at a street kiosk, or a frozen patty six-pack in your local supermarket.

But of course, for a super mopane burger, there's nothing like home cooking. Here's our recipe of the month from Mrs Elizabeth Starling of Hazyview:

500g part-grilled mopane mince
1/2 tablespoon of melted butter
1 teaspoon grated lemon rind
1/2 teaspoon sesame seeds
Dash of tomato sauce
Salt and pepper to taste
1 tablespoon soda water
1 egg, beaten
1 cup dried breadcrumbs
1 tablespoon butter

Method
Combine mopane mince, melted butter, lemon rind, salt, pepper, sesame seeds and tomato sauce. Stir in soda water and shape into patties. Dip each patty into beaten egg, then into breadcrumbs. Place in heated butter and fry for 10 minutes, turning once. Place patties in oven-hot rolls. Serve with tomato-sauce, mustard and banana chips.

This month's competition: 'My chili con mopane'. Recipes, please.

Your Family, April 2005

In 1960 there were 2,5 billion people in the world. Now there are over 5,5 billion. In 60 years' time, the United Nations predicts there will be more than 10 billion. And we all need food.

Today, 750 million of the world's population suffer from malnutrition. The Human Science Research Council reports that nine million are South African children who 'are exposed to the risk of impaired physical and mental development'. Meanwhile, food mountains perish in order to stabilise prices. Food supplies are not insufficient; people die of hunger because they cannot afford to eat.

Famine is exacerbated by transport problems and the lack of a world food reserve system. Great increases in agricultural productivity also put the world at risk. Only 15 plants account for 75 per cent of the plant calories now consumed. In breeding for yield, genetic variation suffers. New diseases and pests could create a global food crisis. Domestic animals supply 150 million metric tons of meat each year. While technology may help the yield to grow, their grazing lands will diminish.

The world demands more food at lower prices in less growing space. The increased productivity of current food sources is part of the answer. But we would never have reached the Information Age by making carrier pigeons fly faster. New thinking is needed; even if it is a rediscovery of old wisdom.

edible insects and robert kok

Of what use are bugs and worms in the universe? To begin with, they're an edible, nutritious and extremely cost-effective food source. World-wide, 1 462 species of edible bugs have been reported and digested, with no serious side-effects. Famine-prone countries in Africa such as Somalia, Sudan and Mozambique do not have an insect shortage. One swarm of locusts weighs 30 000 tons; most of it protein.

Grasshoppers as a delicacy are featured in the Bible. Ancient Greeks and Romans favoured locusts and beetle grubs, feeding them grain to fatten them. Today in Zaire you can feast on fried caterpillars; in Japan and Korea cooked wasps are a delicacy. New York fast-food (or should it be slowfood?) now includes earthworm omelettes.

Korean farmers have turned grasshopper-collecting into a business. Pesticides once destroyed South Korean rice-field grasshoppers. In 1989 a group of farmers stopped spraying to grow organic rice. Today, baked hoppers on boiled organic rice is a popular, eco-friendly dish.

In Mexico the locals eat 308 different kinds of insect as well as drink a few in their tequila. Specialities include fried scorpions and ground-up water bugs in hot pepper sauce. At cinemas in Columbia, you wash down roasted ants with coke, while the French send their garden snails around the world.

At banquets held by the Explorers' Club in New York, honoured guests are offered beetle bars and roasted crickets with their cocktails. They then dine on chocolate cricket torte, honey bee soufflé, insect quiche, mealworm ganoush and waxworm fritters with plum sauce.

Chinese sushi
If raw fish seems a trifle obvious nowadays, try a new culinary adventure. Go to Phat Ho for live Chinese water-bugs. Pick them out of the water, and as you try to eat them, they in turn try to eat you. May the best man, woman or bug win!

The Star, February 2005

Those in the know describe insect flavours as 'nutty' (ants and grasshoppers), 'buttery' or 'bacony' (caterpillars and worms). 'Mushrooomy' and 'potato-chippy' are other taste experiences.

In southern Africa, locusts, flying ants, caterpillars (especially mopane worms), sand crickets and many types of beetles are traditional delicacies. But city-slickers don't seem interested.

For the more fastidious of us who would prefer prawns piri-piri or lobster thermidor to fried waxworms or baked hoppers, it may be discomforting to know that crustaceans and insects are very closely related. They belong to the same group – the arthropods – because they have jointed legs as adults. Although they scuttle around the ocean floor eating refuse, arthropods are a culinary treat. But once they step outside the water, the jointed-legged ones plummet down the social scale, even though they are more nutritious than most foods on supermarket shelves.

The nutritional value of bugs is similar to beef, but gram for gram, it takes far less grazing land to fatten a bug than a cow. Insects are 'ectothermic', meaning their body temperatures fluctuate with the environment. They don't burn calories to stay warm, and so convert a greater portion of the food they eat into food you can eat.

Nor are they as fussy as cows about what they graze. In China, pollutants such as coffee pulp are being fed to beetles and flies whose larvae, in turn, provide cheap high-protein feed for livestock and fish.

Robert Kok, an agricultural engineer at McGill University in Montreal, believes bugs can be the answer to world hunger. He has a plan to build factories that would raise insects in 'true industrial quantities'.

Each factory could supply 10 000 tons of bugs a day for processing into simulated burgers and chicken breasts. Kok estimates that 100 of these factories, strategically placed around the world, would supply much of humanity's need for protein, reducing famine and replacing our dependence on meat, fish and chicken.

have you eaten a bug today?

Quite possibly. Although you may never have deliberately eaten an insect, you probably have accidentally consumed over a pound of bugs in your lifetime. Flour beetles, weevils, and other pests that infest granaries are milled along with grain, ending up as minute black specks in your piece of bread. Small grubs and other tiny insects can be found in your fruit and vegetables. Insects are common in canned food and certain beverages. For instance, bug infested apples in commercial orchards usually end up as cider. You have swallowed a bug or two — and lived. And instead of harming you, the innocent, lowly regarded bug did you good by providing extra protein in your meal.

healthy chickens and three-kilogram carrots

Healthy chickens strut around the veld and in the farmer's yard, growing up to four kilograms. The meat is rich, dark and delicious.

The chickens we eat today come from the chicken factories. They rarely weigh more than two kilograms. Their flesh is pale and bland. The factory chicken eats grain while healthy chickens dine on insects in the bush. Food for the factory chicken must be grown and processed; food for the healthy chicken flies and crawls in its immediate surroundings.

Is our factory chicken a symbol of progress? If more unused land were given over to healthy chickens, villagers would have a source of income, veld chickens could join Karoo lamb in good food guides, and bugs would make a noble contribution to the food chain.

Earthworms do their bit for humans and the environment if you train them to be compost makers. Feed them food waste, animal waste (dog droppings included), garden waste, soggy paper and cardboard. Or, for a real treat, cow manure and sewage sludge. One kilogram of earthworms will process 0,5 to one kilo of organic waste in 24 hours.

The earthworm droppings, called castings, make what is claimed to be the world's best plant food — helping to produce metre-long cucumbers and three-kilogram carrots, palms that grow 25 per cent faster and flowers that are more colourful. The plants are more pest-resistant and need less watering. Naturalists as diverse as Aristotle and Charles Darwin have praised this humble worm.

In America you can buy a starter pack of earthworms and a bin for their castings through the post. With 1 000 worms you have your own small worm farm. They make rabbits look lazy. Your initial thousand, if they're prime four- to six-month-old breeders, should become

800 000 in 12 months. After 24 months, under ideal conditions, they theoretically multiply to over 800 million. That's a Texan-sized worm ranch.

Urban farming is a survival strategy throughout southern Africa. Problems include lack of water, poor quality soil and the abundance of pests. Could waste and urban worm farms put more food on the tables of the poor? As well as being ecologically correct, the earthworm is also politically correct.

the mopane worm factories

While the 100 Robert Kok mega-insect factories are still an agricultural engineer's dream, mopane worm factories are a business reality. For millions of years they have been built by Nature.

Throughout the Northern and Eastern Transvaal, spreading through the Kruger Park to Mozambique, you will find the mopane tree. It thrives in low-lying land despite poor alkaline soil and erratic rain. In the heat of the day, the large leaves fold along the mid-rib, conserving moisture. They look like thousands of resting butterflies.

The leaves taste and smell of turpentine. They are favoured by buck, elephants and a fat, hairless caterpillar known as the mopane worm. The mopane is a child and parent of the emperor moth, high in protein, vitamins and minerals. They are chewy, with a piquant, nutty flavour. The worms can be roasted and eaten hot, or boiled in salted water and spread out in the sun to dry. Then they are stored.

Mopane worms, also known as African viennas, grow plump during the summer rains and then are collected in their millions. Brought to the factory wholesalers, they are boiled and bagged. Then they go to cafés, trading stores, general dealers, spazas and hawkers. The mopane worm market is estimated to be in the tens of thousands of tonnes – the economic impact, in rural areas, is considerable.

'Number One' is a low-cost chicken product made up of entrails and a few heads and feet. During winter, the sales soar; during summer productivity drops as rural populations, especially Northern Sothos, enjoy their traditional delicacy. There are growing fears that the worm is being over-harvested; in parts of Botswana they have disappeared and in Zimbabwe armed gangs rob rural women of their worm harvest.

The production of mopane worms could be industrialised. We need large-scale, production-line thinking and marketing. Where is the Henry Ford of worms?

Worms! Yuccch! We turn our heads away from this age-old and cost-effective source of protein. Increasing affluence, as well as world dominance by French and Italian recipes, banish the creepy-crawlies from civilised tables and thought. Although they are represented in Mexican and Chinese indigenous cooking, bugburgers are rarely featured in cookbooks.

They look revolting; not half as revolting as a kingklip, but then whoever looks at a whole kingklip, with skin, fins and hideous face? We see perfect fillets that have been fried in batter on the cover of a box in the supermarket deep freezer. That's edible.

Worms have to change their image. They can become the foot-soldiers in a war against malnutrition. With the right appearance they could even become fashionable.

prawns of the sky

In Thailand, where crickets are a delicacy, they are called prawns of the sky. In Mexico City swank restaurants offer *tacamoles*, less romantically known as fried teenage ants.

Sushi sounds more palatable and more expensive than raw fish; ditto *escargots* versus brown snails.

South Africa has edible worms. Can the ad industry that enlisted ostriches to sell greeting cards, sheep to sell a TV channel and a white mouse to sell a car find a way for worms to sell themselves?

The target market is debatable. The first strategy is to be direct and feed the starving. Then we must talk to the United Nations, the World Bank and the World Health Organisation for funds, as well as food companies like Nestlé, who must be persuaded that worms can save the world.

The second strategy is to make worms more acceptable. Begin with the more adventurous chefs who would try diced mopane as stuffing in a marrow or free-range chicken. Disguise it in loaves and stews.

Kids who put frogs in their pockets and watch dung beetles for hours would probably welcome, with the right campaign, worms for tea. If you start with the young, you eventually modify eating habits and prepare for a world population that is growing at 250 000 people a day.

In the new millennium the worm and bug can share a new destiny, joining the soyabean as saviours of the human race.

Fried mopane fillets and chips
1 Roll mopane fillets in breadcrumbs and deep fry
2 Serve with tomato and onion sauce and deep-fried chips.

Mopane tortilla
1 Marinate mopane in lemon juice and virgin olive oil
2 Bake in oven for 5-10 minutes
3 Serve in tortilla with guacamole, salsa and sour cream.

Viva mopane
1 Serve mopane worms wriggling and fresh on mopane leaf
2 Squeeze worm out of skin and tickle its tail with a dash of tabasco
3 Eat leaf and worm
4 Wash down with a double tequila.

The Mopane Quick 'n Easy Cookbook, 2005

fourteen
adventures in cyberspace

The people speak

'My name is Margaret Dlukulu. And this is Tshidi, my granddaughter. I am here to have my say.'

She is 74, she told us, her back bent by almost 60 years of gathering firewood.

'Then five years ago we got electricity and I lost my job. It was about time.'

She had come to the community hall to vote on a regional proposal to ban all toxic waste. This was her fourth visit on the issue. During the first three she and her granddaughter had sat at the computer, taking interactive lessons on the subject. As Margaret is still learning to read and type, Tshidi helps her.

'And we discuss it together,' she says, 'but the vote is mine. The young one cannot vote until she is 15.'

Should the motorway running through Khayelitsha be ploughed up to make market gardens, sports fields and swimming-pools? Do the residents of Aberdeen want to become permanent actors in a Karoo theme-town? Issues, large and small, are being debated every day outside parliament and council chambers by the people they affect. And not only debated; they are voted on. Computers bring issue education and participation to the people.

renaissance dawning

> In town and village halls, schools, colleges and training centres, networked 'Aware' programs spread the issues to everyone interested, then collect their opinions. These interactive programmes feed back the opinions to the policy-makers. Although the people's choice is a guide rather than a mandate, brave or foolhardy is the politician who ignores it.
>
> 'Aware' has been funded for the last five years by a consortium of American and Japanese companies with backing from their governments. It is not a corporate feel-good gesture. South Africa has been chosen as the world test market for high-tech democracy.
>
> Internatter, August 2007

By the year 2000 there will be over 200 million users of e-mail and the Internet. There will be 500 million computer users, approximately 10 per cent of the world's population.

Over 50 per cent of computer sales are for domestic use; in the USA, the personal computer now outsells the TV. In South Africa, one million people are already on-line. World-class information technology businesses are being born here. Whilst this country has never been competitive in the Industrial Age, it could be a leader in the age of gathering, filtering and sharing digital information.

computer ears

Electronic surveys are everywhere on the Internet. Before you buy anything or even start looking, you are asked a battery of questions from your age and income to how many overseas holidays you put on your credit card in the last 12 months. For organisations, it is the most cost-effective way of receiving feedback – as respondents supply their answers digitally, the information can immediately be analysed. What's your opinion on the latest Washington scandal, who's your favourite soap-opera star, do you like the taste of new extra-nutty granola – the surveys can be tiresome, but if there is something in it for the customers, many will play along.

Are these surveys statistically accurate? That depends on your target market; and feedback can never be harmful as long as it is a guide rather than a dictator.

What's the coolest home page on the Internet, and what's the most popular? What are the demographics of U2 fans and stamp collectors. What is the psychological profile of a goldfish lover? On-line questionnaires are going to multiply, creating databases that will be cross-referenced to target you as a fish-loving U2 fan interested in single parent life insurance (now including, at no extra charge, a goldfish cremation scheme with the ashes of your beloved pet in a ceramic celestial bowl that plays 'Still haven't found what I'm looking for').

While computer ears enable commerce to become more personal, they will also allow local and regional governments to enter a meaningful two-way dialogue with their constituents. To begin with, local interactive systems will operate in high-income towns such as Aspen and Colorado. People can sit at home sipping high-balls and complaining about vagrants on the ski-slopes. It will be the Aristo.net. If you have the money and the time, your voice will be heard.

We also need the democrat.net with a community focus on those who have never used computers and who are never expected to. If the voiceless majority can only have their say once every five years with a cross on a piece of paper, they will grow disillusioned and cynical.

A community feedback program would start amongst the 'tekkies' and the youth. To increase the level of participation, we would need a 'Help your community; have your say' campaign, with computer-phobes being lured into the town halls, corporate centres and classrooms by children who earn free educational game-time for every new user.

The programmes will falter when policy-makers are slow or half-hearted in feeding back their responses. But if people know they are being listened to, the initiative will work. Communities can become more involved in their own welfare. School stayaways, bond boycotts, robberies and violence will be countered by strategies that are shared, not imposed. Literacy will increase; jobs will come from local ideas rather than national dreams.

Facilitation centres, like the Carter Centre in Atlanta, exist in the USA to bring different minds from different social strata together. All participants can input their ideas on computers reporting into a network program that instantaneously clusters responses. Street gangs have stopped their wars this way, and 50 American admirals decided, without hand-to-hand combat, who was going to lose which ships in the next Pentagon budget cut.

High-tech democracy has its limitations. If you ask 'Should we have the death penalty?', you generate intense emotions, and it could be incredibly difficult for a government to ignore the result. That turns our rulers into order-takers, and the last of the good minds would leave government to the bureaucrats, pension-pushers and power-hungry. But if you want feedback on, for instance, 'Should rural matric students study Shakespearean tragedy?', or what contribution your province is going to make to World Environment Day, the answers will be enlightening.

The democrat.net process will give you information about the issues then pose questions that probe understanding. After this, you electronically fill in a five to 10-minute questionnaire.

The methodology is not new. In the 70s, Sweden asked its citizens to decide on the national nuclear policy. Any citizen who attended a minimum number of education sessions was allowed to vote. Democrat.net will be accessed by personal computer users who pay a small on-line fee, as well as community users who are given access free of charge.

Computer ears can penetrate airports and hotels, servicing tourists and business travellers who are encouraged to share their opinions of service levels. The results would be analysed and fed back to the service providers as well as training institutes that teach the value and benefits of world-class service.

Prototype computers, cars and toasters can be designed and redesigned on-line, with potential customers contributing their criticisms and ideas. 'CAD' used to stand for 'Computer Aided Design'; in our interactive age it will become 'Customer Aided Design'.

Listening to your customer is the first rule of business and government. Reacting speedily to what you hear is the second rule. Cyberspace makes it possible. Now no one is unreachable.

a trip to the cybermall

On the Internet you can buy a pair of Levis straight from the United States, or a coffee-grinder from Prague. All it takes is a couple of mouse-clicks and a credit card number. You can send flowers anywhere in the world, choose silk boxer-shorts from Brooks Brothers, steaks from Omaha and gold rings in antique designs from the Metropolitan Museum of Art. There are discount computer, book and record stores in the Cybermall, alongside the Cadillac Electronic Showroom, diamond bracelets and world cruises.

By the year 2000, there will be hundreds of millions of potential shoppers in cyberspace. That doesn't mean the real malls will be deserted. Far from it; customers enjoy the tactile, in-store experience. It's an outing, an opportunity to see and be seen and to be part of the Sandton City, Westville Mall or Tyger Valley community. Yet if Cybermall can capture only five per cent of retail sales, it becomes a multi-billion-dollar opportunity.

Access to Cybermall will be denied to most South Africans who do not have a computer, modem and a monthly budget to access cyberworld. The local market, for retailers selling to individuals, will not be a lucrative business for the next few years. For South African companies, two opportunities exist. One is the business world. Globally, it is estimated that until 2000, at least, 80% of Internet trade will be business to business. You can order cars and copy paper in bulk, tighten your logistics, and sell to IT-friendly professionals.

The second opportunity rests with South African entrepreneurs who identify global niche retail markets. They can access the world with a good idea, paying most of their costs in rands, while receiving most of their income in dollars, euros and yen. As Microsoft, AOL, Yahoo and Amazon.com race to build the Cybermall of cybermalls, a global retail niche becomes a prize catch.

co.za! south africa's high five in cyberspace

Global Cybermall rates five cool co.za stores:

1 The universal biltong company
More macho than peanuts, more sociable than hot dogs and more

versatile than fish fingers, biltong has gone from ox-wagon to starship hyperspace. With guaranteed delivery within 48 hours of order. As one net-ad says: 'Beam me up, biltie'. South African communities in London, Sydney, Perth, Toronto and Dallas are global biltong's unofficial ambassadors.

Flavours include beef, ostrich, eland, crocodile, kudu and kangaroo. Japanese grade one beef biltong, made only from hand-massaged cows, is now served with Western Cape lobsters on the yachts of the rich and reckless.

2 Afrika, Afrika

The glorious colours, natural fabrics and loose-fitting styles of Africa are street-wise and ethno-chic. 'Afrika, Afrika' is a cyberspace fashion co-operative aimed at the fashion-conscious 16 to 25-year-old. Designers take traditional clothes such as the *dashiki* (a long, embroidered West African top) and give it a twenty-first century flavour. Girls wear new-age *dashikis* as mini-dresses to matric dances, accessorising them with workboots. At Afrika, Afrika, African ethnic meets trip-hop. World-wide delivery by FedEx.

3 Ebony soul

Hand-carved chairs and chess sets made from sycamore, mahogany and ebony; woodcuts representing township life, spiritual experiences and legends; animals carved from driftwood; great soapstone sculptures; limited editions of rhino and wildebeest for sunless skyscrapers; paintings of Cape Town and deserts. African art is ridiculously inexpensive in global terms. One half-decent Hockney could pay for a wall of Pierneefs, Gregoires and Saolis. Exhibiting in the cybergallery gives local artists world exposure, while collectors surf from the heart of Africa to Alice Springs in search of the next Picasso.

4 Inter-Africa-active

Why spend 10 days in a run-down rondavel on a littered beach, when just 35 kilometres away you can have paradise? 'Inter-Africa-Active' will show you 1 000 amazing destinations in southern Africa on CD-ROM.

This is Africa as rough, or as refined, as you want it to be. Click to view the hotel, bedrooms and diningroom. Peruse the lunch menu, watch an interview with the hotel manager. Dougle click to go surfing, mountain climbing, river-rafting, or gliding through the Okavango swamps. Test-drive Africa at home, then book through Inter-Africa-Active in the cybermall.

Their property section takes overseas investors on guided tours around beautiful homes and neighbourhoods. Any places in Plettenburg Bay with a wine-cellar and gym? Click, click.

A new section features in-depth profiles of southern Africa's sporting prospects. The 'Soccer Scene', updated every six months, is now requested by 80 per cent of all European major league soccer clubs.

5 HAT (Herbal African teas)

HAT offers a range of 15 herbal infusions, created by a group of *sangomas* (traditional faith-healers) from the Transkei and KwaZulu.

Their newest hit is a blend of sweet herbs and leaves that help you slim. Internet-nauts are humming the jingle while they surf:

*'If your tummy's fat ...
just drink your HAT'*

*Bubbling under from co.za!
'Ou Van's Handmade Hunting Knives'
'Blow-Up Hippos and Crocs' inflatable pool toys.*

Strings, 2007

adult edutainment machines

The ATM sits outside a bank dispensing cash and little else. The Adult Edutainment Machines (AEMs) will sit inside a store and provide interactive point-of-sale information. AEMs are multimedia kiosks that support (or even replace) salespeople by showing a fashion customer seven ways to accessorise a cream linen skirt, taking a prospective car-buyer on the Monte Carlo rally or demonstrating the versatility of a new drill to a do-it-yourselfer.

renaissance dawning

The AEM can also train and motivate sales people, taking them through the frequently asked questions, showing ideal merchandise layouts with a featurette of the achiever of the month.

Well-funded schools and technikons will invest in these machines too, giving their students 24-hour access to quality teachers with infinite patience. You didn't understand that last equation? Just touch the screen and she will take you through it again. And again.

The key to the success of these machines is their edutainment value. Electronic catalogues and droning professors are not much fun. Once the novelty of touch-screen interactivity wears off, the kiosks will gather dust unless the software has a creative spark.

But how do you create an interesting program that can be seen and heard in random order? How can you have a storyline or a tempo? It's a marathon for a copy writer, too piffling for a film-maker, and production costs often mean the end result is little more than a brochure with a voice-over.

It is still a new industry and amongst the flops there have been a few successes. 'Frozen tomatoes' is an interactive science lesson that shows tomatoes cannot be frozen. You interact with an animated version of a Jerry Lee Lewis absent-minded professor, and you participate in the experiments, using the mouse to pick up a beaker or set the temperature of a bunsen burner.

Another award-winning program was made for the museum kiosk at the San Jacinto battlefield. You can follow tactics; you are shown what it was like.

Being there amongst the ghosts of those that fell is an enlightening and emotional experience. Cape Town Castle, Rorke's Drift, Blood River, the Great Hole of Kimberley, Pilgrim's Rest, Gold Reef City and Londolozi Game Lodge – South Africa has the raw material in abundance. Can we make the tourist AEM a commercial proposition as well as a creative triumph?

home alone

On the Internet, you travel the world without leaving home. Performing research for this book, I found out about worms, gold, adventures in cyberspace

low-income banking, Tanzania and ethics with a click or two of the mouse.

The Internet is a wondrous maze of information, knowledge and foolishness. Powerful search engines take you on a journey from things you wanted to know to universes that you never knew existed. For the lonely and the curious it is an endless, self-absorbing loop.

For the cyber-worker, it is the freedom to work where you wish to live. In virtual teams, the camera designer can live in Thailand, the lens engineer in New York, the electronics expert in Cape Town and the project manager in Berlin. They meet on-line to generate ideas and share progress. If the lens engineer suddenly decides to take a year off to go roller-blading, the project manager simply calls up the Cyberspace Personnel Agency for a replacement. Working where you wish to live will see cyber-workers migrating to havens of connectivity, beauty and peace. Why live in a Johannesburg suburb when you can be near the beach in Noordhoek, or on a houseboat in the Miami swamps?

Multimedia software is becoming powerful in the education arena, and as the concern for public schooling escalates amongst the world's middle class, in-home edutainment could be the 'killer application' CD-ROM promoters seek.

The Microsoft encyclopedia, Encarta (a name created by computer), is a CD that replaces 29 volumes of text. It has over 14 000 moving pictures and diagrams as well as seven hours of sound. Animation demonstrates how bees communicate, how to waltz and explains quantum theory. You can see cheetahs run, Satchmo play and presidents being shot. Hear TS Eliot and Allen Ginsburg read their poetry, 200 samples of world music, speeches from Kennedy, Churchill and Gandhi. Edutainment often takes a multi-user, multi-learning approach to one subject. *A Whale of a Tale* is an animated children's story, with songs and stories about whales, as well as games, colouring-in books and music. Our five-year-old son proudly faxes to his grandfather the report generated by his pre-school CD-ROM.

BBDO in New York predict that 70 per cent of American home-users of multimedia computers will employ them mainly for educational purposes.

renaissance dawning

This huge and growing market is fuelling a software explosion. Expect CD-ROM platinum sellers ranging from Noddy in Multimedialand to Harvard business professors strategising on your laptop.

Quality software in turn makes a multimedia computer a must-buy, especially in a home with children. In South Africa, it is becoming the pre-teen status symbol. Your kid won't go over to Bella's house, but not because she's black or white. Shame, the poor child doesn't even have multimedia. Of course, the kids may not be studying. I remember hiding *Dan Dare* under *Advanced Geometry*. Now Doom 2 hides under the multimedia quark. You can challenge yourself in gameworld or go on-line, become Ozymandias, king of kings, and take on the gamesters of the universe.

The Sierra Network is dedicated to games. Laid out like an amusement park, it is divided into several lands. First you build up a face, like an identikit, that represents the character you want to be. Then you can play chess with a Martian from Nevada, fight the Red Baron or enter a world filled with on-line magicians, monsters and trolls.

Locked in this imaginary world where no one is who they are, it is easy to forget that your real family and friends exist. Just as television changed social habits, so does the personal computer. Television reduced socialising and hobbies; it rearranged the living-room so that chairs and settees faced not each other but the box. However, the TV room was still a family meeting place where some interaction took place and decisions were made, if only about what to watch next. The personal computer demands privacy, small dens instead of open spaces, an interaction between human and machine, or between two or more humans through the machine. The personal computer is not family-friendly.

> 'When he says "Wake up, baby" or "Good night, honey", he is not talking to me; he's playing with his voice-activated computer. He spends all his free time with it; his wife and baby hardly exist.' KAREN G

In the past, families grew up having dinner around a table. Then we started to have dinner in the TV room with trays perched on our knees. Now it is take-aways in front of computers for literate family members, while the non-literates laugh to themselves in front of the TV or go out to find others who can empathise.

Wrap-around dark glasses and headsets are being developed by Sega, Nintendo and Sony to give you totally private virtual reality. You could go shopping in Harrods, or make love on a beach in Hawaii. No one but yourself will know. Your isolation will be complete.

the mufamedi family dinosaur show

The computer, multimedia and the Internet have injected interactivity into the couch potato. Now leisure life is slightly more demanding than the occasional flick of the remote.

It is time to marry technology with family values. Here is an evening in the near future:

> Benjie Mufamedi came home from school with a dinosaur project. At 18:30 that evening, Benjie, his parents and younger sister, Martha, gathered around their family teleputer, otherwise known as their TP. They had the 70 inch split-screen model with full remote controls, double-modem and the 24 CD-RaR (Read and Record) loading tray. Benjie had been hard at work on-line since 16:30, electronically bookmarking 15 of the most interesting dinosaur sites.
>
> During this first evening of the project, the Mufamedi family looked at the sites and talked strategy. The title was 'Dinosaurs of the Karoo', and as Benjie's mother pointed out, the sites were all dinosaur specific. Although some mentioned the Karoo, a search for 'Karoo: Origins' could give everyone another perspective. Benjie's father used the split-screen and double modem to compare two animated recreations of the bradysaurus. Martha recorded the recreation of the bradysaurus bark, sampled it on her synth and started to lay down the first track of her dinosaur quartet. On instructions from his teacher, Benjie called a halt at 20:30. There were to be five more family dinosaur sessions over the next month, then Benjie would present the Mufamedi Family Dinosaur Show to his class. His parents would, of course, make a copy of the CD-RaR to show the family at Christmas.

With a TP in the home, education becomes fun – a family thing. What you learn is less important than how you learn it. It is the current fashion to talk of work teams and virtual teams. Cyberspace and multimedia could give us something infinitely more valuable – the family team. For five evenings a month, multimedia learning becomes a family date.

Of course it's unfair; the gap widens between haves and have-nots. Yet, whatever the price, a teleputer will be a fraction of the cost of private schooling. That means many more families can afford it. In this 'have and have not' world, education takes a small step towards democracy.

Meanwhile, a multinational computer company with deep pockets and a culture of ubuntu will develop big screen, interactive multimedia that is affordable. It will go into the classrooms and training rooms of the developing world, allowing teachers to become mentors, sharing the learning process. It exists now, at a price. It allows specialist teachers to interact with classes in different places. Aborigines in the outback present their art to buyers in Sydney. An aid worker in Somalia tries to comfort the starving while a United Nations official sitting in Geneva watches her. Then she turns to confront him, on-line, in their teleconference, and he has no place to hide.

> Life is a little easier now, Margaret Dlukulu told us. Instead of collecting wood, she grows flowers around her shack.

> 'I love them so much; they are very pretty, and I make some good money. I grow the flowers for the flowersellers.'

> (Leaving town on a Friday evening, a motorist hurriedly stops to buy some flowers on the side of the road. It is township to suburbs trade.)

> This month, the farm school that Tshidi, her granddaughter, attends bought two computers. Half the money was raised by the community and half came from local government. There were concerts given by the school, and market days, where Margaret Dlukulu sold her flowers for the computer fund.

> 'Half from you, half from us' was last year's big issue in the 'Aware' program. The final vote was an emphatic 'yes', and these two computers are the first harvest. On week days they are used by the children, on weekends they are used for training the unemployed; in the evenings they are reserved for the workers.

In the meantime, Margaret Dlukulu comes to the town hall every month. She is not important to the politicians only once every five years. She can regularly stand up and be counted for the things she believes in; she has her say.

She sees the results on her local television station. Often the politicians and the people agree with what she says, but not always. This month the subject has been toxic waste. Next month they want to know about women's rights. Margaret Dlukulu laughs: 'Some things you can change by voting, but you can't change men.'

Tshidi tugs her sleeve, 'Grandma, we can change anything.'

fifteen
siyabonga

Mandela Pappendorp opening for Xmas!

The ninth Mandela Holiday Camp in Pappendorp, the Western Cape, will 'definitely, absolutely open in time for the Christmas holidays' claims MHC chief executive, Horace Nxasana. On the banks of the Olifantsfontein River, Mandela Pappendorp is the fourth holiday camp to be built from scratch; 'and we haven't missed a deadline yet' says Nxasana.

The first Mandela Holiday Camp opened in Durban, February 2000, by taking over an army barracks. Since then, the Mandela formula of low-cost vacations and family entertainment has given over 100 000 South Africans their first taste of a true holiday.

Tourism.co.za, August 2006

Tourism is the largest foreign exchange earner in the world, and the world's largest employer. Out of every 15 people employed, one works directly or indirectly in the tourism industry. World-wide, it accounts for six per cent of the gross national product (GNP). It is also the fastest growing industry around. The aging baby boomers of America and Europe are joined by the new jet-setters of the East and the globe shrinks as air-travel becomes more affordable.

South Africa has sun, scenery, beaches and animals. It is affordable when you have dollars, euro or yen. So why is our tourism industry a relative disaster?

As an earner of foreign exchange for South Africa, tourism comes in at a poor fourth accounting for about three per cent of our GNP.

In Australia, tourism is the fastest growing industry and largest export earner. Tourism there creates five times more export earnings than tourism here. Accepting that both countries have beaches and good weather, if Australia does so well on kangaroos, Ayers Rock and an opera house, South Africa could be netting a few billion more with lions, elephants, mountains and Cape Town.

Australia has the advantage of being neighbours with Japan and the new wealth of the East, as well as with bored New Zealand sheep farmers. Tourism from Africa will never make South Africa wealthy; our target markets in Europe, Asia and America all have closer options. And in Australia you don't lock yourself up at night to avoid being blown away by an AK47.

But once you've seen one kangaroo, you've seen them all.

stretch targets and strategy

In the decade between 1994 and 2004, world tourism will double and revenues will triple. South Africa started far behind. To become a major contributor to economic prosperity, the South African tourist industry needs a stretch target – and core strategies to achieve it.

A stretch target is meant to do what it says ... stretch. Another name for it is a BHAG (pronounced bee-hag), a Big Hairy Audacious Goal. Is the following Big and Hairy enough?

Year	Overseas tourists	Gross export earnings
1994	704 000	$1,9 billion
2006	6 million	$15 billion

Six million tourists is not meant to be an easy target; that's what stretch is about. Yet it is possible. While world tourism quadrupled in the last 25 years, here it stagnated. If South Africa had not been the polecat of the world, tourism could already be our number one export earner.

129

How do we come to earn $15 billion a year? A Harvard Business School wisdom is that only three strategic options for a brand, a business or an industry exist:

- cost leadership
- differentiation
- focus.

Cost leadership means you produce your product or service profitably for less than your competition. South Africa can do this for its domestic market by creating holiday camps that put fun before luxury.

Differentiation means you maintain a product or service that offers unique and competitively advantageous features. And we can. Southern Africa has been blessed with a full pack of wildlife from the big five to warthogs, whales and eagles.

We have cultural diversity, good weather, beaches and wonderful scenery. So do many other countries. Animals and game reserves set us apart. Everything else adds to the experience by creating a comprehensive range of attractions. The core of our differentiation strategy is animals plus.

The focus strategy demands that you identify a marketing niche in which you are better qualified to serve than any other competitor. A high-spending niche is the international jet-setters of the Northern Hemisphere. Their winter options are ski-ing or travelling to the other hemisphere. Cape Town, Rio and Sydney are the main southern contenders, and of the three, Cape Town can be positioned to offer the most elegant fun. From November to April it can be a non-stop top-drawer party.

Any strategy, however elegant, doesn't put a bottom on an airline seat. To earn $15 billion a year, we need to understand our target markets, package our destinations, create new facilities and most of all change our attitudes.

tourism, like charity, starts at home

If more South Africans became tourists themselves, our future service-givers would experience first-hand the delight of good service and the

siyabonga

disappointment of bad. How can the average South African afford to take a holiday? Simple ... make the holidays affordable. Create fun-filled, subsidised holiday camps.

These African holiday camps could take inspiration from the Billy Butlins Holiday Camps that flourished in the UK after World War II. Converting disused army camps (and there are quite a few of those here), Billy Butlin created holidays for the working class. Although the accommodation was by no means luxurious, there was non-stop entertainment during your stay and the Butlins red-coats were always around to make sure everyone had a good time. Much of the entertainment was provided by the holiday-makers themselves. Early morning exercises, talent shows, beauty contests, soccer and volleyball tournaments, bingo evenings, quiz shows and discos – the pace was relentless. The red-coats would jolly you along every waking moment, and families returned year after year for their week or two of escapism. British workers left their council flats and grey skies for Nissen huts ... more grey skies ... and a low-cost, fun-filled holiday.

Translated into the 21st century, South African holiday camps will have more good weather than bad, high-tech games, Internet access for all, choir contests ... and most of all, unique opportunities for families to experience a holiday together. For urban parents with rural children it would be a time to treasure.

Who will subsidise these camps? Businesses that want to incentivise their lower-paid workers. Corporations that would like to offer holidays as prizes for initiative and effort. And leaders in the tourist industry who want everyone in their employ to experience what a good holiday is. For how can you give good service until you have received and appreciated it? Sponsors would be recognised as enlightened employers and can expect this investment in their people to be rewarded with enthusiasm and health as the campers return to work happy.

animals feed people

Sun City is a marvellous destination, but it will not motivate millions to travel half-way across the world. Nor does Ndbele design, Zulu beadwork or a shark-safe beach in Margate. You can find all of it somewhere else. But nowhere else has our variety of game and game parks. The Kruger National Park is the world's most diverse and best-run national game reserve. Surrounding the Kruger are hundreds of lodges, ranging from simple camps to luxury hide-aways. We have game farms deep in the heart of KwaZulu-Natal, in the Free State and less than two hours' drive from the centre of Johannesburg. A short airtrip away, the Okavango, Kariba, Kalahari and Namib take you to some of the last places on earth where humans are still guests in vast animal kingdoms.

We need to make this differentiation deeply relevant in people's lives.

Basically, three kinds of international visitors come to game parks. First there are the 'click-it, tick-it, next' brigade. They arrive on their high-speed guided tours and demand a list of animals in the reserve. Then they go on their game-drive with a ranger, speeding from animal to animal, stopping just long enough to click a camera shutter and tick one more species off the list. If there are not enough ticks at the end of the two hour drive, they feel cheated and complain. But tomorrow is the great hole of Kimberley and the morning after, a trip up Table Mountain. Click-it; tick-it; next.

These visitors are unlikely to visit a game reserve more than once in their lives; they've done the elephants and rhinos and the Amazon's waiting. Yet there are enough of these 'click-it, tick-its' for South Africa to flourish. They need reserves close to airports because 'click-it, tick-it' tours depend on a minimum of travelling and discomfort. The proposed Gauteng reserve around Bronkhorstspruit, an hour from Johannesburg, will be ideal. The main lodge must be world class, with an ethnic flavour: 'click-it, tick-its' expect a Hilton in the bush.

The second type of person is the traveller rather than the tourist; a person who searches for spiritual meanings and experiences, as well as relaxation and the perfect lobster. Travellers will not see every room in the Uffizi Gallery, but they will sit for hours in front of a painting that moves them. And they will remember a chilled glass of chianti at the trattoria on the square of a small Tuscan village.

To travellers escaping high-pressured, air-conditioned lives, the bush will bring a measure of inner peace. There are less travellers than *siyabonga*

'click-it, tick-its' in the world, but they stay in a place longer and return more often. Southern Africa will need more Londolozis and Mala Malas, as well as upmarket time-shares that offer the world traveller a home in the bush for a week or two a year.

The third type of game park visitor is the business traveller. Either the 'three days in Johannesburg, two in a game farm and home' frequent flyer, or the 'last year it was Hawaii' convention-goer.

How can a warthog on its front knees or mock-fighting buck help business people and convention-goers find common ground? Wildlife takes us out of the here and now. Watch a herd of rhinos making their way to a waterhole and you are transported to an age before human beings walked the earth. Were the *bosberaads* before the elections positively influenced because human disputes seem more petty in the bush amongst the animals?

Most game reserves that claim to cater for conventions of more than 20 people have meeting rooms less inspiring than a dentist's waiting room. A quick game-drive followed by eight hours of noisy air conditioning, stack-away chairs, greasy chicken and soggy vegetables are not the ingredients for a memorable convention. If we want to tempt the 100 greatest life assurance consultants of South Korea or the Sony multimedia world development team, we need to make the conference in the bush a mythical experience. As well as twenty-first century facilities, the reserve could have facilitators that compare and contrast the behaviour of wild animals with life in the concrete jungle.

Convention-goers are great spenders. Many have platinum expense accounts, while others who have already paid for their trips have wallets rippling with traveller's cheques. Alongside big and small convention rooms, we await an exclusive chain of afrocentric boutiques that offer quality clothes and art, coffee-table books and visuals of animals on CD-ROM, all with intercontinental delivery.

'Click-it, tick-its', travellers and convention-goers all require wooing. Satour needs a decent budget and a highly imaginative communication system. Television commercials and programmes showing wildlife may charm, excite and shock viewers, but they rarely, if ever, evoke the awe and peace of being there. Conveying how animals spiritually feed people will be a great challenge.

Wild animals physically feed people too. There are plans to double the size of the Kruger Park within the next decade, reaching far into Mozambique and giving villagers there a reason to finally stop their on-again, off-again wars. Ecotourism has the power to turn guns and death into wooden animals and guided tours.

Animals are not, except for true believers, an 18-day experience. They are the jewel not the crown. Imaginative packaging will make southern Africa a multi-faceted destination.

Top five 'Wildlife & More' Holiday Packages
See the greatest herds of rhino left in the world, play golf on the edge of the Indian Ocean and have personal consultations with a genuine tribal witchdoctor.

Experience the three wonders of southern Africa: the Lost City, the bush and the unspoilt beaches of Mozambique.

The big five or your money back when you stay at three of our 'Travellers' Choice' game lodges for a total of eight nights; plus free casino chips.

For the ultimate African adventure skydive off Table Mountain, bungee jump over the Victoria Falls, go white-water rafting, track a lion and swim with the hippos.

Extract from Wildlife & More Internet site, July 2006

the cape escape

Cape Town is one of the world's natural play-centres, especially from November to April. The mountain is awe-inspiring, the coast is fascinating, the vineyards add class as well as provide legendary lunches. It is a walking, meeting, eating, seeing and being seen, relaxing city. This is international territory where, in season, the duke's son and assorted debs throw Möet around in Blues, while father holds court at the Mount Nelson. And Swiss bank accounts buy homes from Llandudno to Paarl.

Yet Cape Town has the potential to be far more than a play-pen for the rich and scandalous. It can become a centre of twenty-first century Western civilisation during the long northern winter. An artists' city, it is one that inspires with every view out to sea or up to the mountain.

Cape Town also has problems. The major one is that it doesn't work very well. The World Bank has called it one of the most inefficient cities in the world. In terms of safety, Cape Town ranks alongside Rio and far behind Sydney, and no one is sure whether things are getting better or worse. There is added pressure on the city because outlying small towns and farms are collapsing economically. Unemployed, homeless people create a ring of ghettos built out of disease, poverty, crime and anger.

Another problem is that most Capetonians, apart from hoteliers, are not really interested in tourists. They barely put up with the influx of Gautengites at Christmas. Tourism is the price they pay for living there and, like most humans, they would like to pay as little as possible. They are happy to export their fruit and wine, but no one really wants the mob to descend for a jolly, rowdy holiday.

The place and the people have to change, but not radically. Cape Town is not a mass market venue (Durban does that better). It can be a market niche for the cultured and well-heeled of the world.

To service them best, Cape Town needs to de-pressurise. The cultural élite will have their own holiday homes or be house-guests. Those on the vast cultural fringe do not want air-conditioned skyscrapers. They can have that anywhere. Instead, Cape Town is developing its own stylish versions of the French *pensions*, offering bed and breakfast for up to 20 guests. These *pensions* will be centred in up to 100 communities in the greater Cape Town area. Cape Town is a city of communities; each with its own flavour. From a mall to a farm-stall, each has its own version of a town square, with a few specialist shops and restaurants. And each has a range of accommodation to satisfy the residents and guests. A community could contain 200 tourists and 1 000 residents. Two hundred residents would be directly employed by tourism, with another 400 indirectly involved. These smaller-sized communities encourage people to meet and become friends – the best guarantee for repeat business.

Venturing from these home bases, Cape tourists are offered a diversity of attractions: long, elegant lunches in the winelands, promenades along waterfronts, rides in theme-parks and on beaches, whale-spotting afternoons in Hermanus, talent-spotting evenings in Clifton and a summer-long festival of the arts. This festival can showcase contemporary and traditional music, drama and arts of the world and Africa to create a unique annual event. And hosting the cultural élite is something that Capetonians may even enjoy, especially if their only alternative is more noisy Gautengites.

The re-planning of Cape Town is taking place. This is the time to make it the sophisticated city of the south, taking advantage of the world's biggest and fastest growing industry. But pressure from the poor and homeless will only be relieved when the small towns and hinterland become economically viable, perhaps by concentrating on satellite services and products for the tourist industry. Cape Town needs to grow smaller before it grows bigger. It needs to become safer and cleaner – the cultural élite won't put up with danger or dirt.

By focusing on a summer cosmopolitan market, many Capetonians will only have to work hard for half of the year. And instead of trying to persuade everyone that Cape Town is lovely in winter (which it actually is), the tourism industry should take their holidays from June to September. The animals and Mandela Pappendorp will be waiting.

creating the capability

Tourism will only become South Africa's biggest export earner and employer once there is national commitment. It is potentially the most important seat in the cabinet, deserving the best brains the country has to offer.

Business has pledged R1 billion to stimulating employment and most of this money will be invested in tourism related projects. The time has come for a small visionary task force representing the community, the environment, labour, industry, financiers and government. These visionaries must have the power to make a difference. They must plan for the next century. How can our airports handle six to ten million tourists a year? How can we bring in meaningful foreign exchange while keeping venues affordable for locals?

We need to build world-class tourism facilities. In the UK there are huge subtropical swimming, leisure and entertainment areas sealed under double-skinned geodesic domes. In Key Largo, Florida, you can spend a long weekend below the waves in the Jules Verne undersea lodge. Guests dive down to the dry, ventilated hotel (a converted underwater research lab) while their luggage is delivered in a waterproof canister.

The governor of Amazonas has proposed an eco-theme park; an ecological city with buildings in clearings connected by raised passageways, while animals circle underneath. Others propose high-tech living capsules made of inflatable, transparent spheres for the ultimate eco-weekend.

In the Caribbean, cruise-liners have bought islands that they populate with a couple of bars and approved 'locals', to give passengers a safe, ethnic experience. In Minneapolis, the shopping mall has become a holiday destination. The Mall of America covers 78 acres (over three times the size of Sandton City) and includes a seven-acre theme park as well as six hotels. In South Africa we already have the Lost City. Is the next world-beater on the drawing-board?

In the meantime, what will we do about tourist safety? A recent survey reports that five per cent of British tourists get mugged in South Africa. When more people realise that crime and violence harm us all, there will be less shelter for the criminals. Visible policing has dramatically reduced crime along the Durban beach front; and surveillance cameras are catching criminals in the act along the Cape Town waterfront. But while gang warfare in the Cape and brutal hijackings in Johannesburg grab world headlines, many will stay away.

Other surveys reveal that overseas tourists rate South African service as near the world's worst. We are often too servile, too arrogant, or simply uncaring. After you experience Swiss and German efficiency, French flair, Italian friendliness, Japanese cleanliness and American customer orientation, the local offering is a confusing and half-hearted mess.

value the guests of africa

If you are a company with a sub-standard level of service, you will not go far with a 'give a better service or you're fired' attitude. It is more helpful to look for shared values, give relevant training, encourage step-by-step improvements and find a flag to march under. Then the journey begins.

South Africa Tourism (Pty) Ltd is an under-performing company. It needs a decent budget; but first it needs to adopt a set of shared values. Here are some that deserve consideration:

WE VALUE UBUNTU AND LEARNING.

- By helping each other we help ourselves. Together, we encourage more tourists to visit us.
- Tourists to this country have been to many others. We learn from them.
- The sharing of mistakes can be more constructive than a focus on successfully done functions.

WE VALUE INTEGRITY AND EFFORT.

- If we see crime happen and do nothing, we are like the criminals.
- Giving bad service to tourists and taking their money is being a thief.
- The more service we give, the better off we will be.

WE VALUE FAMILY AND FRIENDSHIP.

- A family must feel safe on the streets of our cities.
- If we can become friends with each other, we will be friends with the world.
- Let us celebrate our differences and embrace our similarities.

WE VALUE AFRICA AND THE GUESTS OF AFRICA.

- We borrow the land from our children.
- Africa can change people.
- May all our guests take home a little of Africa in their hearts.

siyabonga

We need an emotional flag, a unifying thought that symbolises the new, tourism-friendly South Africa.

Visitors enjoy learning at least one phrase of the country they are in. And that phrase is usually 'thank you'. In Italy we learn to say *grazie*, in France *merci*, in Portugal *obrigado* and in Greece *efharisto*. The words themselves resonate. And in South Africa there is a word that easily equals them: *siyabonga* (pronounced say-a-bonga). Just saying it brings a smile to most people's faces.

Today, we can start saying *siyabonga* to our guests and each other. It will be shared by Afrikaners and Zulus, Indians and Vendas. You could hear *siyabonga* with a very English accent at the Rand Club, an Italian inflection at the suburban pizzeria, a Portuguese lilt at the local greengrocer's and a clink of glasses in the local pub. *Siyabonga* will add to the word travellers' lexicon, spreading the desire to visit our country and people.

Tourism should put bread on millions of tables in this land. It must reach out to remote farms and fishing villages as well as into township squatter shacks. Nature has given us the opportunity to create wealth and keep our land beautiful. The time to do it is now. *Siyabonga* Africa.

sixteen
the Joburg jol

Global travel shifts

From Honolulu to the Cape, surveys show that people are spending less time on the beach. The hole in the ozone has turned sun-tanning into a death-wish.

The new Asian, Chinese and African tourists have better things to do with their yen, yuan and rand than change skin-colour. International youth don't want to share beaches with bawling three-year-olds. And the 50-somethings are bored with sand between their toes.

The seaside is losing its charm. The new trend is to go straight from your city to someone else's, especially if it has these twenty-first century winning options:

- pleasant weather for most of the year
- no obvious pollution
- entertainment – day and night
- multiple options for activity and relaxation
- a high degree of safety
- good opportunities to meet people
- some kind of ethnic experience.

The sea, for all its attractions, is becoming an optional extra.

worldtravel.com, September 2004

the joburg jol

Onassis once gave a persistent journalist his three rules of making a fortune. They are:
- Live at the best address, even if it's in the basement next to the boiler-room.
- When you borrow from the bank, borrow big.
- Show off a sun-tan all year round.

Rules one and two may still apply; rule three has been turned on its head by the ozone layer. Skin cancer is neither smart nor chic, and acquiring a sun-tan is fast becoming an act of stupidity. Who wants to do business with someone so careless about life?

In fashionable New York restaurants and clubs, the palest of faces are the most socially acceptable. And even in California, the over-bronzed look is interpreted as short-term thinking.

Asians and Japanese have never been sun-worshippers. African tradition has equated sun-blackened faces with agricultural labourers. Now the ozone hole emphasises what everyone except the palefaces already knew – soaking up the sun is a stupid way to spend your time.

While companies compete to sell the longest-lasting, least allergenic block-outs, people will reconsider their holiday options. Rather than the best beaches, they will look for the best fun.

Who in their right mind would consider Johannesburg?

gauteng is where it's gappening

South Africa is a growing nation. Only war and disease can prevent consumer demand from increasing. Even in our rural areas, the numbers will rise dramatically, from 12 million in 1985 to 16 million in 2010.

While most of these 12 million people had no water, electricity, rights or television in 1985, most of the 16 million will have at least three of the four by the year 2010. In the high road scenario, rural areas will hum with activity.

Cape Town will be throbbing in 2010 with four million residents and a few million tourists. Durban is busier, with six million residents

renaissance dawning

plus tourists, and a growing Indian Ocean trade that will keep a chain of container ships out at sea filled to capacity.

And Gauteng will roar. The engine will be powered in 2010 by 16,5 million people. That is more than double in 25 years. Sixteen-valve Gauteng will be the megacity of Africa, where most business will be conducted and fortunes made. Banks, mining houses, multinationals and most of the South African top 100 are in Gauteng. The province will house over 20 per cent of South Africa's population in less than two per cent of her landspace.

What happens in Gauteng determines which beer, chewing gum, washing powder and car southern Africa prefers. Gauteng will pump out music and TV programming for a continent, transferring its kind of 'cool' to the African world. At the heart of it all is Johannesburg, the city of gold – a great place for business, but can it also be fun?

'Johannesburg is the commercial heartland of the province, the country, the subcontinent, and sub-Saharan Africa.' TOKYO SEXWALE

can joburg be a jol?

Imagine. You live in Johannesburg and you have friends from New York or Paris coming to stay. What on earth are you going to do with them?

Until recently, the choices were bleak. After a couple of shopping malls, a flea market, and Gold Reef City, there was nothing much left apart from the braai circuit. Within a couple of days you pack them off to Sun City, Mpumalanga or onto the Blue Train, muttering, 'Cape Town is a great place for a holiday, but we couldn't live there'.

Now there are more Johannesburg options. Open-air cafés have sprouted around malls to make Rosebank and Sandton Square the places to be seen. A busy waterfront and lake appeared as if from nowhere. Pubs and clubs in the suburbs, taverns and street parties in the townships, make entertainment and socialising more relaxed and affordable.

You can find Mexican and Indonesian cuisine rubbing shoulders. You can take away sushi and bobotie. The steaks are still Texan-sized, the seafood is as fresh and more varied than at the coast, and there's a reasonable Italian restaurant in every suburb.

The Market Theatre complex is a multi-cultural centre. The theatre district has spread from the renewed Civic Theatre to Kyalami and Midrand. Cinemas show everything you can see in London and New York, apart from re-runs of Warhol's *Man Sleeping* and all-night Japanese monster movies. Private art galleries in the suburbs display the best of Africa and world art. The Crocodile River Ramble takes you out of town and into the workshops, studios and gardens of artists and craftspeople. Have tea and scones surrounded by soapstone sculptures. Or a pizza made by a watercolourist.

Shopping as entertainment ranges from world-class malls to makeshift stalls on busy pavements and flea-markets that include the organically correct as well as the African and funky.

Legal casinos have come to town and the area around the Carousel is a theme-park in waiting.

The climate is sports-friendly. Visitors can play tennis and golf all year and enjoy unheated pools for six months. Gauteng hosts world-class cricket and rugby matches nearly every week in world-class venues. In most cases, the spectators don't freeze or become soaked with rain. While English football fans may still look down on local skills, Kaizer Chiefs versus Orlando Pirates has as much passion, music and colour as Liverpool against Manchester United.

But Johannesburg has become a dreadfully violent place. Death is casual; guns are as common as shopping bags. And as the violence continues unchecked it seems that everyone, black and white, has a horror story to tell. Without safety, the social fabric disintegrates.

safe – from *a* to *b*

However, the vast majority of people manage to go about their business peacefully. Across the suburbs and even in the city centre there are many islands of safety, but Johannesburg lacks efficient ways to interconnect them. The city of gold's transport system is pathetic – no intra-city rail system; a dangerous minibus taxi industry that most whites, through snobbery and fear, elect not to use; a bus system that

renaissance dawning

ignores life's new realities and cars that have become targets of hijacking.

There are also glimpses of light:

- People are beginning to park and ride to sports events and concerts.
- Adventurous northern suburbanites order minibuses to and from a night on the town.
- Private bus companies ferry passengers between airport and hotels.

To make the Johannesburg Jol happen, we need transport options that recognise the dangers of twenty-first century city life. These should offer a range of comfort and price levels. And there is no budget for overhead rail systems or subways.

Here is a beginning:

- Rapid transport buses will feed through the centre of town and network all the islands of safety, day and night.
- Pick-up and drop-off points will be well-lit, small hubs of activity.
- Taxis will offer various levels of customised service – there is the minibus you hail on the street, the radio-controlled Corolla that takes you from door to door and the Camry with a chauffeur who carries your shopping.

This is a holding pattern; Johannesburg needs public transport that is effective, a pleasure to use and a spur to CBD investment. The answer that has already being proposed is the 'light rail transit system'. In other words, hi-tech trams that run on rails. They offer more comfort, more reliability and a better image than anything we have at present. They are also highly efficient at transporting people. In the rush hour, the trams can run 90 seconds apart with one line moving 20 000 people an hour. The best buses will do is 12 000 per hour. Hong Kong uses light rail to cope with its almost impossible congestion, American cities choose it for all-round appeal and German cities consider light rail to be the environmentally-friendly way to travel. Rubber wheels were fitted to the German trams, making them so quiet that hooters and bells had to be added.

Residents become fond of their new trams, and in different cities around the world they have been given nicknames such as the 'Transit', the 'Trolley' and 'Max'. Developers like the system too; the routes are collecting points of potential customers. Three years after Max started in Portland, new development on the routes exceeded $800 million.

Taxi owners will resist light rail, but they can be allies rather than competitors, feeding into and out of the main routes. And taxis cannot cope with congested routes such as Louis Botha Avenue, the road from Alexandra to the centre of town. There are 328 people per hectare in Alex; that makes it as crowded as Hong Kong. Light rail cannot do anything for living conditions in the township, but it makes leaving and returning a quality experience. The proposal for light rail has been on the table for some time; the buck has been passed to the new local authorities. In the meantime, no one has had a better idea that is remotely affordable, and transport chaos sparks more crime.

Once travel is easier, there will be more places to travel to. When there are more leisure and pleasure opportunities, there will be more people who are attracted to them. Venice without its bridges and New York without yellow cabs wouldn't work. Sometimes it's surprising that Johannesburg does.

what is a cape foot?

Johannesburg is not a big city, but it is still a town-planner's nightmare. Other cities in Africa all have main streets wide enough for an ox-waggon to turn in. Johannesburg began as a mining town with no wide streets and city blocks the length of 200 Cape feet.

Traffic doesn't flow well in central Johannesburg. You find a succession of streets going the wrong way, and the rigid grid structure makes going across town a laborious, truck-blocked process. We need a few bold diagonals and broadways to open the city, making it bigger and more relaxed. One broadway can curve from Joubert Park through to Westgate Station. A second can link Newtown with the city and suburban stations. These broadways will cross around the City Hall and the old post office, which is becoming Gauteng headquarters. And a third broadway can feed in from the Wits University campus.

renaissance dawning

These diagonals, making a five-pointed star, will create a centre of attraction when they are joined. London has Trafalgar Square; Johannesburg also has pigeons, and an opportunity for our own Nelson's Column where the roads meet.

When groups march in Johannesburg, whether for protest or celebration, they have nowhere to march to. If Nelson's column stands in the civic spine at Rissik Street, it can be balanced with our own *Arc de Triomphe* spanning Rissik Street in front of the Civic Centre. In this utilitarian age, the Arch of Democracy must have a useful function. As well as being a rallying point and an entrance to the city, it can be the African Trade Centre and a hotel, its broad legs straddling the Rotunda and a convention centre built over Park Station for 2 000 gold-card delegates. Johannesburg must begin to look and feel like the great city of Africa it is destined to become. The Cape foot must be kicked out to make way for the African block.

making a theme-town

To change perceptions, Johannesburg needs an outright winner. Cape Town and Rio both have the mountain and sea, Florence has art, New York has the buzz and Hamburg has red lights. Johannesburg has trees, space and Africa. That's not enough; the rest has to be made. The brief is to create a place to see and be seen; a place filled with interesting people, where you can hang out, meet and be entertained. It is a cosmopolitan experience with a taste of Africa. And if possible, build on what there is rather than start from scratch.

It *is* possible. Drama, jazz, painting, dance, photography, museums, art galleries, theatre workshops, libraries and all-night raves are transforming a derelict area. There is a good pub and restaurant, and the selection of retailers is interesting, although limited. The Market Theatre is already well-known; that's half the battle won. Now it needs to be redeveloped to turn the Newtown Market into a legend.

See Africa in Africity
Off Afrofashion Avenue there is Gold Row. Walk down Arts Street to Sangoma Crescent. Or stop at an outdoor café around Turbine Square. There are street

bands, artists showing portfolios and young actors giving patrons a taste of the plays currently on stage.

Inside Turbine Square is the heart of Africity; food, fashion, art and fine jewellery are made and traded from the stalls and open-plan work spaces perched above.

Stroll through Premier Arcade, where the original Internet Espresso puts you in touch with the wired universe, and the Video Diner displays the music of Africa. If you want to work out, there's a gym with windows looking onto the street for maximum visibility pecs-flex. For the less energetic there is the wine and biltong bar ... and a pub that stocks beers from every country in Africa.

Plans for three new apartment complexes between the Newtown Market and the Oriental Plaza have been approved. The winning architects are a group of Malawi, Ndbele and Zulu women who combine traditional styles with organic and synthetic building materials. Their creation of cowdung, fly ash, perspex and deconstructionist Ndbele is awaited with great interest.

worldtravel.com, September 2004

Making a theme-town is a bold endeavour. It is the central vision of a city that believes in itself. A redeveloped Newtown will balance business and pleasure; new and old, local and global culture. There are over 40 hectares that can be part of the vision. Can you change an abandoned market, potato sheds, a power station, mills and hostels into the cultural and artistic soul of Africa? History says 'go for it'; the area has re-invented itself more than once before.

the newtown soul

Newtown began in clay and swamp. The clay attracted a polyglot society of brickmakers during the 1890s. It was a rough and ready shanty town filled with a rainbow society of unskilled burghers, African labourers and Cape Malays, together with the poorer immigrants from Europe, China and India.

Brickfields was the earliest centre of social integration on the reef. The squatter camp grew daily, and the huge clay pits became the town's refuse dumps. To bring some order to the mushrooming chaos, a parcel of stands was made available at low rentals to poor Afrikaners, and Burghersdorp was born. It was still a cosmopolitan area, drawing together the poor of all races who lacked mining skills. The clay pit dumping grounds had become massive disease breeders, and in 1904 pneumonic plague broke out. Burghersdorp was declared an unsanitary area, there were forced removals and the Indian location was burnt down by the fire brigade. A young lawyer, who helped many to fight expropriation and who nursed victims of the plague, was shaped by events like these for his life's work. His name was Mahatma Ghandi.

The town of the burghers developed again – this time as Newtown. In 1911 the new market was built; the largest structure under one roof in southern Africa.

Newtown supplied fruit, vegetables, grain, livestock and power to Johannesburg. It was a working-class area and a hub of protest against capitalist excess. In one confrontation, a group of women led by Mary Fitzgerald sat on the tramlines to stop scab labour from running the trams. The police used pickhandles to break up the protest and Mary Fitzgerald, in later demonstrations, used a pickhandle as a symbol of harsh and meaningless force. The Newtown car park that transforms itself into a market is named after her.

From the 1960s, Newtown went into decline as Johannesburg grew. The city needed more than the old area could provide. The markets, mills and power stations moved to empty suburbs. The powerplant had run out of steam. By the early 1970s, the markets were the homes of ghosts, gangs and tramps.

Meanwhile, a cultural awakening was percolating in a Yeoville flat. Mannie Manim started a theatrical experience that found vibrancy and relevance in the struggle of being together in a separate society. In April 1975, 'The Company' was awarded a bigger home; the Market Theatre began the next rebirth of Newtown. For many years The Company fought a lonely battle. On some nights there were twice as many on stage as there were in the audience. They persevered, and slowly around them something unique in Africa began to grow; a place simmering with cultural enthusiasm.

This has not been happening by accident. History, geography and a dedicated group of cultural revolutionaries are making Newtown a world-class attraction. Without adequate funds or consistent political support, they have secured the area with what one of their leaders calls 'cultural squatters'. Artists' co-operatives, theatre groups, dance, video and TV studios, a jazz centre, a workers' library and an overseas cultural institute can enjoy low rents, an uncertain future and the opportunity to create a legend.

Does Newtown have a future? South African Breweries think so. A few years before their centenary in 1995, the company decided to create a museum and looked at a 150-kilometre radius around Johannesburg before they decided on its location. Their R25 million investment focused on Newtown.

There are ambitious plans for the redevelopment of Newtown that would make it a place to live, work and enjoy. Thirty thousand affordable homes can be built to the east if the decision-makers agree to make a decision. An empty hall can come back to life filled with stalls, shops and workshops. There are problems to overcome that include noise pollution from motorways and northern suburb paranoia. Corporations such as Old Mutual, the Post Office and Premier Milling, who own key chunks of the 40 hectares, must be significant players in the development or they must sell without being greedy.

To push this ball over the line, we need an eight-man scrum. And it won't be easy. Will veterans of the struggle approve millions for a museum, while around the back their comrades squat on a dumping ground in homes made from black plastic garbage bags?

Do we need to pay millions for art while, around the corner, street children try to escape a life of glue-sniffing, prostitution and petty crime by going to a makeshift school that cannot afford to give them pencils? If art and culture are to receive public money, their champions must offer rational as well as emotional arguments. Can an investment in Newtown profit the residents of Gauteng in ways other than spiritual? This is a mining town, not Florence or even San Francisco. Can the poor profit from something that is good for the soul?

At the opening of the first Biennale, 4 500 people filled Mary Fitzgerald square. Once again nations of the world mingled, gossiped, did business and enjoyed themselves in old Brickfields.

Yet after the first night, the exhibitions did not receive the audience they deserved. On many days, security guards outnumbered guests.

renaissance dawning

Perhaps the marketing was too reticent and élitist, while getting there was not a pleasure. The second Biennale, more obscure in its selection of art than the first, drew even fewer visitors.

Even if the show manages to capture public imagination, only when dedicated transport links with northern suburb islands of safety give secure day and night access can Newtown live again. Right now it needs to reach a critical mass. Newtown is the place best positioned in Africa to become the cultural centre of new ideas and old wisdoms; a melting pot for a country and a continent.

clubland and other jols

There is a street in Istanbul where prostitution is legal. On one side, shops display their wares from trapeze-swinging Swedes to the large and lovely in black chiffon. On the other side, cafés serve double-strength Turkish coffee with sweet, sticky baklava. The street is patrolled, regular medical checks are carried out and the use of condoms is strongly encouraged.

Hillbrow is selling sex all the time. Drugs and muggings are part of everyday life. While it may never again be a safe place for pensioners to walk their dogs, if sex is legitimised and violence curbed, Hillbrow will be the naughty-but-nice red-light district of the Joburg Jol.

London's Soho has a thousand ways to make you part with your money. It made Paul Raymond (of Raymond's Revue Bar) the richest man in Britain. You can enjoy sleaze without having your throat cut or a .45 thrust in your face. If you mess with the London mafia you acquire concrete boots. Otherwise, you'll make it through the night.

In gun-packed South Africa you need far more protection. The theme-streets of Clubland define the limits. By allowing the sale of sex, the risk of disease and death are lessened and criminals are marginalised.

There is something else Johannesburg needs to give it life. The Victoria and Alfred Waterfront has transformed Cape Town. Other seaside cities and towns, from Durban to Knysna, are hurrying to build their own. The Thames and the Seine created London and Paris; Geneva has a lake; Sydney has a harbour; the Joburg Jol needs water.

The flea market and restaurants around Bruma Lake (resembling rather a large puddle) have been followed by the Randburg Waterfront. More ambitious water-based schemes utilising dams from Wemmerpan to Jet Park should develop. Major retailers and hotels will join market stalls, restaurants and bars, creating open malls built for the Highveld rather than for Canadian weather. Local needs, the environment and national pride will finally slow down the wholesale import of overseas experiences.

Water should also feature in the hot, dusty townships. Public swimming-pools, alongside basketball courts and football pitches in multisport centres, will provide the youth with healthy alternatives to street corners and video arcades.

Major sporting arenas such as Ellis Park are ready to become multi-use facilities. The rugby field can be used for the under-15's Gauteng schools' final as well as for rugby tests. The hallowed turf becomes an attainable dream. Ellis Park should also offer a rugby hall of fame. We need one, and it will give the stadium a new source of revenue (unless Loftus beats them to it). Newtown and Ellis Park situated on the east and west sides will form the cultural and sporting dumb-bells of the city. In between, other plans have been hatched. Jewel City would be the heart of mineral beneficiation in Africa, with a manufacturers' and training village adding value to gold and jewellery. On top of Park Station we can build the convention centre that the city deserves.

The Johannesburg city centre has six million square metres of developed floor space, well over one million of them standing vacant. Plans have been passed for two million more. If the Joburg Jol starts in earnest, we can have 50 per cent more people working in town, and the council will earn 50 per cent more rates from business. The returns are there if crime and grime are dramatically reversed, the investment is made and a unique character is encouraged. Johannesburg can be a vibrant part of the global village rather than a poor copy of somewhere else.

To the south there are plans to create a spectrum of medium- and low-cost housing aimed at young homemakers that would bring Johannesburg and Soweto together. If this rainbow project were to happen, the Joburg Jol would become a true reflection of the changes occuring in the country. To the north, a greatly revamped Lion Park, farmsteads with Michelin star lunches and big horizons, Magaliesburg farms offering weekends of milking cows, riding, climbing and bush-lore, will give city dwellers a taste of Africa.

gauteng.com

Make the best Gauteng contacts:
Business, academic, sports, cultural.
Network with Africa before you get there.
Log into Gauteng.com . . . now!

The Internet is creating cyber communities of people with common interests. It is both a meeting place and an information centre where the trivial and serious, the sacred and the profane, the wildly profitable and struggling rub shoulders. It is the ideal place to start the Johannesburg Jol.

Cape Town is on the net, as are small American towns in Arizona that are targeting the retirement community. Where is the hub of southern Africa? The Johannesburg Stock Exchange is represented, and the Biennale, while it lasted, was a lively net-spot. Wits University has a bare bones entry, and that's about it. The world's most inquiring minds with global access are ignored by a city and a region whose biggest problem is self-confidence in the world market-place.

The various Gauteng chambers of commerce are grappling with how to present the hub of Africa to the world. Gauteng.com will be a newsgroup, a shopping mall, a place to make business, cultural and social contacts. Travel agents will include the home page address of Gauteng.com with every ticket to southern Africa. Travellers will conduct business and build relationships in advance from half-way around the world.

The best thing you can hope for when visiting a new city is a friendly face or two, even if you have never seen the faces before. A common interest in wire coat hangers or the a cappella style of music can blossom into friendship. Or at the very least result in a pool-side braai, complete with beer, an umbrella and block-out.

NorZu star in Africity street bash
Last night NorZu sent the 25 000 guests of the opening of Africity into wild leaps and frozen poses with their warrior music.

NorZu are a young Norwegian in silver latex and an old Zulu in animal skins. As the Zulu dances, the Norwegian stands completely still. Her latex bodysuit glows to the rhythm and their street-bash anthem 'Hep' blasts out of 200 speakers. Nor's silver suit is coated with sonic transfer, translating the movement of Zu and her breathing into music.

As NorZu climaxed their act with three storey holograms of themselves projected in front of Turbine Square, Nor spoke her only words of the night: 'Welcome to the century of Afrocentricity.'

Worldtravel.com, September 2004

johannesburg update

During 1996, Thami Nxasana and myself were invited to facilitate a process for the Johannesburg inner city that engaged all relevant stakeholders and elicited a shared vision. During the process it became clear that Johannesburg has the capability of becoming the leading city of Africa. The essence of the vision is: Johannesburg, the golden heartbeat of Africa, is a dynamic city that works.

The vision demands that Johannesburgers take pride in their city; that crime and grime are dramatically cut back; that shared strategies, tactics and resources keep the process on track and that political infighting does not derail it. On all counts, the jury is still out.

seventeen

it's better than Bournemouth

Dear fellow church members and friends,

It is now two years since we arrived in South Africa and came to our lovely retirement village in Sedgefield. And we're still enjoying every minute of it. The village looks out over the lakes, and it is only a 15-minute walk to the Indian Ocean. There is a marina next to the Sedgefield Beach Hotel, and six months after we arrived, Harold announced: 'Freda, I want a sailboat. I'll find a chap to give me lessons'.

I wondered if someone had put whisky in his herbal tea, but within two months, my 70-year-old husband had his boat and a sailing teacher, the son of a local boatbuilder. Harold and Alan enter races now and do jolly well.

They take me for a spin sometimes, but I prefer dry ground, especially when it's a garden! Mine already looks very pretty thanks to some expert advice. Our village has its own nursery and greenhouse, developed by six residents who are gardening wizards. Do we miss England? Not very much. The cold and wet weather was making our old bones arthritic; our little house was chilly and damp; and we could feel the pollution clogging up our lungs. Here, winter hardly exists. We are not prisoners of our home and central heating. Life is lived outdoors, making it so much easier to meet people; and when it rains there's always satellite TV. Harold can tear out what's left of his hair watching his beloved Arsenal.

We also run a shopkeeping course organised by our church, called 'Happy Customers Return'. It is very fulfilling to pass on our experience to the locals. We feel we can still make a difference to someone's life.

About ten years ago, when the South London Anglicans went on a coach-tour to Bournemouth, we all said there couldn't be a better place to retire. Well, who could have dreamed of this idyllic Indian Ocean home?

Lots of love,

Freda Hill

PS Vicar Costello, you might enjoy this headline for a retirement village north of Durban: 'Retire to Zinkwazi. It may not be heaven, but it's on the way.'

The South London Anglican Church Gazette, September 2009

There are many worse fates in life than retiring to an edge of the Indian Ocean. And over the next 10 to 15 years, retirement will be the megatrend of the Western world as post Second World War baby-boomers ease into their sixties. It will be the mellow time; time to let go, to exhale and smell the roses and the sea. During their lives, the boomers have changed attitudes and institutions. In the 1950s, schools had to gear up to cope with the bulge. In the noughts, we will see the rapid growth of retirement villages.

Europe, America and Japan will experience the retirement bulge. Not only will more people be retiring than ever before but they are also expected to live longer. Pills and transplants will give millions 20 years or more of retirement. Very few will be able to afford Palm Beach.

world class in africa

World-class retirement villages already exist in South Africa. My father lives in one called San Sereno, near the Bryanston Country Club. Residents occupy 250 clinker-built cottages, each with its own garden. There is also a two-storey block of 50 flats. Facilities include a bowling green, an indoor pool, a restaurant, a library, a community hall, hobby rooms, shops and a frail-care clinic.

The village is made for walking as well as driving, with many common lawns and paths on its 13 hectares. It is peaceful, with views of trees and sunsets. Everyone has his and her own space.

The residents meet while playing bridge, snooker, going on theatre outings, pub nights, doing pool aerobics, walking, feeding the koi and being neighbours. People make friends here. Lunches and dinners are shared, as is a quiet whisky at the end of the day, when chess boards and pieces are taken out and forgotten skills are polished. Residents help each other through times of illness and the death of loved ones. And for people who enjoy travel, their cottage is easy to lock and leave. Even your roses will be watered during your absence.

The village is owned by Sanlam, and is a new concept for the retirement market. The cottages are not sold or let. Instead, clients buy a lifelong right to be a resident at San Sereno. With the money San Sereno buys a life policy and annuity. It is placed in the name of the buyer and guarantees the heirs will inherit the full purchase sum. The sadness of loss will not be heightened by the burden of having to sell a home at a time that is not right for the market. If buyers encounter financial difficulties, they can borrow up to the full amount of the policy.

At the time of the purchase, the levy is contractually agreed to for the lifelong occupancy. The initial levy escalates for a limited number of years, then is fixed. This means residents can budget for life. The levy includes rates, taxes, water, assurance, maintenance, the use of all common areas and amenities, as well as up to 28 days a year free frail-care accommodation.

One of San Sereno's most impressive facilities is the frail-care centre. It caters for 40 patients, some physically and the others mentally frail. It is staffed day and night by qualified nurses and matrons who have more than a diploma. My mother spent the last years of her life there. As it grew dark on the night she mercifully died, the nursing staff came into her room, and, led by Sister Steffie, stood around her bedside softly singing Zulu hymns.

I have seen the long, Dickensian wards of UK National Health hospitals. I have been to a so-called better nursing home on generous grounds just outside London, where the principal care attendant, a large Irish woman with an alcohol-blotched red nose, was a grotesque

it's better than bournemouth

old Punch cartoon come to life. That's the treatment you can expect in England if you are from the middle class, old and ill. If you are in good health, you will find yourself in a small flat or a room in a retirement home, where you queue for dinner.

There are no San Serenos in England. In America there are Florida apartment blocks and retirement centres in small Arizona towns with warm, dry climates. But the combination of comfort, personal space, financial arrangements and genuine care is certainly world-class here, and possibly even unique.

When you have foreign currency, the San Serenos of South Africa are very affordable. You can exchange a small flat in an unremarkable London suburb for a good home and lifestyle in South Africa.

see the kids on showtel

Would people leave their family and friends to start a new life in a new continent at the age of 60? Families are going global nowadays. Most of my father's London friends have at least one child living overseas. People liberated by the Information Age and global entertainment will live wherever in the world they desire. Multinational companies send their hopefuls on far-flung learning curves. Our sons and daughters are becoming an international caravan of affluent gypsies.

This will impact on the retirement decision. You don't know where the kids and grandkids will come to rest, so concentrate on where you would like to be. If you choose somewhere stunning and can afford an extra bedroom or two, you won't have to travel half the world to see family and friends. They will gladly travel, especially in the Northern hemisphere winter, to see and stay with you.

In between visits, you won't have to move from your armchair to see your grandchild take her first tottering steps. You will be linked by interactive video, talking to and seeing each other on your life-size screen.

See the kids on **Showtel***! Every Zinkwazi Retirement Village resident qualifies for one hour of free time every month on the Showtel big-screen, live-video link. Enjoy your grandchildren's formative years and share your new life with old* friends, wherever in the world they are. Showtel's big-screen, live video also has surround-sound, making you feel like you're really there ... and they're really here.

a r100-billion business

In the next 10 years, more people than ever before head towards retirement. And as the world becomes more accessible, options for the aging middle class increase.

International retirement villages around the world will be built in financial security. They can be in rolling parklands, nestled in mountains or overlooking an ocean. They will strive to offer all the facilities of a San Sereno and some may train their nursing staff to provide the care that is a natural part of African life.

South Africa retains a leading set of competitive advantages. Our world-class medical facilities are affordable to the middle class (try having a by-pass in Dallas without platinum-class insurance). We have the space and short winters; we have mountains, the Cape and the warm Indian Ocean.

There can easily be 100 retirement villages along the coast from the Cape to Mozambique, and inland from the Tzaneen forests to the Karoo. Each village can be home to 1 000 residents. To retire modestly and successfully nowadays you need about R1 million. For a Brit, that's less than the price of a decent London semi-detached house.

These 100 villages with 1 000 residents each, bringing in an average of R1 million, would add R100 billion to our foreign exchange reserves. If half the residents were South African, we would still bring in R50 billion. And as new residents replace the old, more wealth will flow to these shores.

recycling the classics

In many societies, the old are treated like toxic waste; you pay to get them out of the way. Traditionally, the people of southern Africa have far more respect for their elders. The elders' advice is sought and their opinions are valued. And so the grey panthers of the Western world can still contribute to society if they live here. We are and will be a nation of the young, ever lacking sufficient teachers and trainers. Whether it is teaching art to children in a farm-school, or bookkeeping to mini-entrepreneurs, the world's elderly can feed the minds of South African youth.

Teaching these classes would be voluntary, with special concessions, like membership at a reduced rate to a medical aid scheme that covers emergencies. Perhaps the teachers could earn 'community hours' that they redeem when they need frail-care or a guest cottage for overseas friends. They will also receive a fair amount of personal satisfaction.

Accounting, legal and marketing services could be offered to charities, stokvels and local businesses. These villages of elders can become centres of good sense and experience. All we need to do is attract the grey panthers who are happy to give as well as receive. As Kevin Costner is told in the *Field of Dreams*: 'Build it, and they will come'.

eighteen
the time-share boerestaat

The men are built like beer barrels with Paul Kruger beards. It is the end of summer, yet it is still hot, and they are gathered around their lunchtime braai, bare-chested, wearing swimming costumes and shorts.

Their wives, in printed frocks, sit on the stoep of one of the holiday homes. The A-frame houses are built around a swimming-pool where their children splash and play.

This is Die Springbok in Brits, a successful time-share game farm where conservative Afrikaners visit their beloved Boerestaat for a week or two each year. Less than an hour from Johannesburg and Pretoria, lying on the drier side of the Magaliesburg mountains, Die Springbok covers 3 000 hectares of poor agricultural land. It is ideal for game and time-sharing.

The land was bought in the 1990s by an Afrikaans consortium, headed by a prominent politician, an army general and Springbok fly-half, all recently retired. First they put up game fences that kept the unwanted from entering and animals from leaving. Then they stocked the farm with buck, giraffes, zebra and ostriches, making it people- as well as eco-friendly. They built houses in clusters, like the re-circling of ox-wagons. Each sleeps six to 12 people.

Die Springbok marketed itself in Afrikaans newspapers as well as at gatherings of the volk, ranging from AWB training sessions to jukskei championships.

the time-share boerestaat

The trio of leaders gave the project the same glamour that Sylvester Stallone, Arnold Schwarzenegger and Demi Moore give to Planet Hollywood. For the Afrikaans faithful it was the promised boerestaat, if only for a week or two each year. The Planet Hollywood experience, in contrast, lasts as long as a hamburger and a Coke.

Phase one of Die Springbok quickly sold out. So did phases two and three. Now prime-time units are going for five times their original price — if you are lucky enough to find one for sale.

'Sometimes I think it would be nice to see the money in the bank,' says an original settler, 'but where else can we be together and be ourselves? Two weeks a year is all my family has left of the dream.'

In the time-share boerestaat you will see no black faces, and there is only one official language. The housemaids, gardeners, cooks and handymen are Afrikaners who had fallen on hard times.

Affirmative action, compounded by down-sizing, left many middle-aged whites without a secure future. The late 1990s were scarred by a rash of white family murder-suicides. Change consultants battled to find ways to give hope to the retrenched. White squatters invaded the farms of their wealthy volk, claiming their race as their right. Farmers then began to see how this new labour force could be used. And so the time-share boerestaats gained their Afrikaans work-force, although some time-share owners are not enthusiastic.

'The new blacks are the poor whites,' says a wealthy, right-wing farmer. 'The only difference is you cannot give them a klap when they are lazy. You must be more civilised to people who go to the same church as you.'

Other conservatives enjoy the Afrikaans environment. 'It shows we don't need any of the others,' remarks a grandmother, cutting up the milktart she has made. 'The blacks, the Indians, the English, the Portuguese, the Jews and Muslims all find comfort in their own communities. And we find strength in ours.

'I'm not saying anything is worse or anything is better. It's just when someone says "shall we have a tikkiedraai on Saturday night?" then everyone knows what the person is talking about. And if I tell the young maid to clean and press my clothes for the tikkiedraai she understands it is important. Then the next day we giggle like schoolgirls when I tell her about the widower Gerhard with his ears that swing like farm gates when we dance.'

Die Springbok faced its biggest crisis when an Indian family applied for time-share.

'We screen all applicants,' says Piet de Waal, chairman of the new members committee. 'You cannot have time-share until you are a member of the Die Springbok Klub. That is the fairest way to protect the interests of everyone here. It is in our constitution to speak only Afrikaans with each other. You can speak your 11 official languages at the Pretoria Show and in the new parliament. We have no quarrel with that. But here we preserve and celebrate our culture.

'The Indian family could speak Afrikaans, but it is not their natural language. They were not fluent enough to join Die Springbok.'

The rejection caused a flurry of protest in the press, parliament and law-courts. Finally, it was decided that privately-funded clubs could control their intake of membership.

'What was the alternative?' a cabinet minister asked. 'By making things illegal we would just encourage clubs like this to go underground, break the law and become more radical. And perhaps it is fairer that one Indian family feels discriminated against rather than the whole of Die Springbok Klub.'

'It would have been war,' says Piet de Waal, as he drove us around Die Springbok in his 4x4. 'Our members' families opened up this country. They suffered and died for it. Women and children were thrown into concentration camps. And then for almost 50 years we ruled. We owned the jewel of Africa. While the rest of the continent went up in flames, we were rewarded by God for 200 years of hard labour, for losing many loved ones and keeping the faith. Is it a crime that we finally prospered? We had no time to correct our early mistakes. Only 50 years, a blink in history. Yes, there were injustices, but did we commit mass genocide like the American settlers who massacred the American Indians? Germans gassed six million Jews and still have their homeland. What do we have?

'Our children face an uncertain future in South Africa. The good jobs are going to the blacks; we whites are now the ones discriminated against. No one talks about that in the United Nations. And no other countries welcome the boer. Only in places like Die Springbok can our children know what it means to be an Afrikaner.

'We created this country. It is in our blood, and our blood has flowed for it. When the ANC took over, they made noises about considering a volkstaat. And that's what it turned out to be — just noise. Ask Pietie, our gardener, whose farm they took to keep some black tribe happy. The Afrikaner had it all. Now if he's lucky, he can spend a few weeks a year in his time-share boerestaat.'

It was lunchtime; time for the braai, a few beers and the silence of the African landscape.

The International Guardian, *April 2011*

nineteen
flowers of the east

Japan's day of love

Valentine's Day in Japan is becoming a time of haiku and chrysanthemums.

It began five years ago when the World Flower Council (WFC) looked critically at its Valentine's Day programme. Asia and Africa were underperforming because the day had never been part of their cultural tradition. WFC decided that the best way to make Valentine's Day global was to think local.

In Japan, this has led to the annual Haikus of Love Competition. The winning entries are published each year in a slim collector's edition, illustrated by leading artists. This, in itself, is a profitable venture for the founders of WFC greetings card division (Japan) who smile (inscrutably) all the way to the bank from their sales of haiku cards.

Some contain love haikus from old masters while others leave space for original compositions. The illustrations provide inspiration and commentary on haikus, both unwritten and written.

To complete the Japanese Day of Love, WFC promotes the gift of perfect chrysanthemums. To deal with the demand, chrysanthemums are increasingly imported. This has significantly boosted the community flower projects in Mpumalanga, as their yields and low capital costs give them price leadership in chrysanthemum production.

> From Hallmark and roses to haikus and chrysanthemums, Valentine's Day is now more universally celebrated than Christmas.
>
> Mpumalanga Herald, 13 February 2005

If problems are the seeds of opportunities, South Africa is a fertile land. Many problems are distressingly obvious. Others with less impact have been hidden in the fabric of an artificial society. Here is one I stumbled across quite by chance.

What can we do with the 25 million tons of fly ash that we produce each year?

Fly ash is the material left over after power stations burn their coal. It travels on conveyors to massive dumps and dams that have become mini-mountains of layered ash and topsoil. Some are partially vegetated. Fly ash is like talcum powder; not really a nuisance unless it blows in your eyes. At the moment, we have 450 million tons of it lying around, mostly in the Mpumalanga. One power station alone, Letaba, produces more fly ash than Australia.

Some of our fly ash is recycled. We have bricks that contain up to 30 per cent fly ash. It is used as a cement extender in concrete and mortar. Fly ash particles displace water between the cement particles, and when water is present, fly ash and cement mixes actually become stronger over time. This makes fly ash a desirable ingredient in pipes and dams, yet less than five per cent of the ash we produce is used. The rest is waste.

Is this a major catastrophe? Fly ash doesn't kill anyone and the mealies still grow in it. It is an eyesore and an irritant. In the scheme of things, it probably would not feature in the 'Top 20 Green Enemies' list. Ash is a minor problem, but it may just be turned into a major opportunity.

fly ash towns

In West Bengal, the Indian authorities have commissioned a $5 million fly ash brick plant that will pump out 80 000 bricks a day, enough for 20 houses, and containing as much as 80 per cent fly ash. Ash for the project – about 200 tons a day – will come from a nearby coal-fired power plant.

Other power authorities encourage similar schemes for the production of low-cost fly ash bricks. India currently generates about 40 million tons of ash a year and, like South Africa, only uses about three per cent of it.

The difference lies in vision. India is planning to use 50 per cent of its fly ash productively, even though new coal-fired stations will more than double the output in 5 years. (It helps that India needs 60 billion bricks a year for housing. That's enough to house most of southern Africa.)

The financial benefit of selling fly ash to make bricks is twofold: the power station earns money and does not have to pay for the landfill. Many American power stations market 50 per cent of the ash they generate, and for every dollar from sales, they save two more.

Fly ash is a subject of world-wide research as governments begin to legislate against waste. Scientists in Australia offer the 'Biofly' brick, a combination of sewage and fly ash that is 20 per cent lighter than clay bricks. Biofly is efficient to produce because sewage sludge creates its own energy, turning itself into the final product in the kilns. Its lightness reduces building costs; for instance, children can help build their new school and learn a skill while they do so.

Then why do we not have fly ash cities? Why can we not reduce the cost of housing? Why do South African bricks have less than half the amount of fly ash of other bricks? Granted, it is an SABS standard, but maybe it is as outdated as the Victorian rule that said an outer wall had to be nine inches thick, the equivalent of two good old British bricks. (In the USA, wooden houses withstand snow and storms. In sunny South Africa, only cement seems to be good enough.)

Fly ash is expensive to transport, being light but bulky. To cut costs, the brickmakers should be situated next to the power stations, with the communities they service close by. This makes the people of Mpumalanga the major beneficiaries; as they live with acid rain from power stations, it seems fair that they can have cheaper, lighter bricks. Except this is not happening. Ashville SA does not exist.

The Eskom ash goes to a company owned jointly by Eskom and the major cement manufacturers. They sell a small percentage, mainly for bricks, dams and pipes, and they are investigating other uses.

flowers of the east

Fly ash comes from coal, whose origins lie in plant life. Burning coal rids it of energy, but the mineral content remains. The ash still has nutrients. In America, sewage sludge and ash are combined to make 'N-Viro Soil', a low cost soil substitute and fertiliser. The ash is usually cement kiln ash, although fly ash is also used.

Toledo, a city in Ohio that pioneered the process, has almost eliminated the costs of sludge disposal, and soon will be making a profit on fertiliser sales. South Africa is short of topsoil, while we have sewage and ash to spare. Our sludge seems to be more toxic than the American variety, and there are poisonous metals such as boron in fly ash. Experiments indicate that when ash and sludge are used to fertilise mealies, the toxicity accumulates in the leaf rather than in the cob. That is acceptable for humans, but not for animals.

In Florida, orange trees are flourishing on an ash and sludge mix called 'Paydirt'. In South Africa, in a five year controlled experiment, a group of pine trees nourished with fly ash grew 30 per cent taller than a group given fertiliser and a third left to their own devices. These pines will eventually be used for mine-props, and so the ash, in a way, will return to its underground home.

If ash is proven to be an effective fertiliser, it may have a billion-dollar destiny – growing flowers. The biggest cash crop in Europe is flowers. The Dutch cut-flower industry is bigger than the South African gold industry. Kenya recently started growing flowers for export, and it has already become the country's second biggest agricultural earner of foreign exchange, the first being coffee.

South Africa already exports flowers to Asia and tulip bulbs to Holland. We have the land, the labour and the power stations that could fill landscapes with colour and movement. Fly ash is alkaline, a natural counterpart to soil damaged by acid rain, and, as it retains moisture, less watering is needed for a healthy crop.

Here is a plan hatched in an evening with a horticulturist over a bottle of red wine, that could, if validated, provide employment for up to 20 000 rural people, with a low capital outlay. It could also create a profitable transport business for anyone who cares to invest in a fleet of trucks and some jumbo jets. Japan and China are rapidly-growing markets for chrysanthemum blooms. By the year 2005, South Africa could supply five million stems a week to the East.

Chrysanthemums need protection and no more than 12 hours of sun per day to bloom. They are usually grown in greenhouses, but in this capital-scarce scenario, let us assume there is no cash for glass.

Imagine a plot of land 100 metres long by six metres wide. Along each side, a few metres apart, a syndicate makes a commitment to its future by planting umbrella tree saplings. It will take five years for Nature's greenhouse to grow and provide shade. The trees must be pruned each year, and portable awnings made of shade cloth will be needed to nurse the flowers to perfect bloom.

In this 600 square metre plot, a syndicate of 10 women can grow, water and protect 150 000 chrysanthemums a year. After expenses they will earn between R1 000 and R1 250 a month each, at current prices. In an area where there is over 40 per cent unemployment, and most of the employed are fortunate to receive R750 a month, this is a good prospect.

To grow five million stems a week, we would need 1 700 natural greenhouses, 17 000 employees, and less than 250 hectares of Mpumalanga. Collection and delivery to the East is an industry requiring refrigerated trucks and two flower-filled jumbos a day. The 'Chrysanthemum Express' will be big business, combining speed and quality control.

All this involves fly ash because chrysanthemums need good soil and water. Sludge-ash is water-retentive, saving our most precious commodity. And it could be the most cost-efficient fertiliser on the market if Eskom so desires. It costs Eskom money to dispose of ash. If Eskom gave it away, or even paid for part of it to be turned into fertiliser, it would be no worse off, the environment would be spared another dump and a few million chrysanthemums would be fed, as would 17 000 families. By 2005 a blend of industrial and human refuse can give South Africa a beautiful half a billion rand export business.

Are these figures accurate? Should we rather grow roses? I am neither a horticulturist nor an accountant, but we have the land, labour, sun and the fly ash. That should be enough. After all, the brains of a computer are made from little more than sand and genius.

the valley of 999 hills

With millions of bricks and millions of flowers, we still have millions of tons of fly ash left over. As well as back-filling mines, ash is used as a multipurpose landfill. In West Virginia, a long valley has been filled to the height of a 10 storey building. Now a shopping mall graces this wide, flat hilltop. A golf course and housing development are other options.

Meanwhile, in South Africa, another power station is due to develop. Majuba, near Newcastle, will offer Natalians almost six million tons of fly ash a year. Be prepared for more ash dams and dumps – unless alternative imaginative solutions are explored.

Much of our farming land has been degraded by soil erosion, while water floods areas like the rolling hills of KwaZulu-Natal, worsening the situation. Can we reclaim land using fly ash and revegetate it? Some may object that the Valley of a Thousand Hills is sacrosanct, but farmers will celebrate the extra pastures. Land can also be used to build a satellite town that takes the pressure off major urban centres, or a small industrial park that brings work to an under-utilised labour force.

Other uses range from ceramics to oyster growing. Oyster larvae become attached to fly ash pellets on the ocean floor, and this underwater farming technique has led to highly successful artificial fish reefs in the Gulf of Mexico. The Chinese already use oysters in their cuisine. Their increasing middle class could make oyster cultivation as big as the 'Chrysanthemum Express', while for the aphrodisiac-hungry Taiwanese, oysters are more plentiful, legal and, presumably, far tastier than rhino horn.

setting a recycling target

Filling valleys, creating artificial oyster beds, bricks and fertilisers enable American power stations, such as Virginia Power, to recycle 65 per cent of their ash. This makes them 15 times more efficient than Eskom.

In 1997, Eskom created 24 million tons of ash, 1 million ton of which was productively used. The only environmental goal that the utility has not met is to '*appropriate targets for waste streams reduction, recycling and re-use*' (1998 Eskom Environmental Report).

Eskom has many environmental concerns that it discusses openly, and its electrification programme is giving a better quality of life to millions each year. In the bigger picture, 450 million tons of fly ash are easily overlooked. Yet if Eskom wants to be regarded as a world-class utility and improve its environmental performance, it needs to set ambitious targets.

Recycling 65 per cent as Virginia Power does, or recycling 50 per cent which is the national objective of India, may be overstepping the mark. How about 33 per cent by the year 2005? It will require radical new thinking, an adequate budget, some research grants to eager universities and the co-operation of communities willing to grow flowers and oysters under controlled conditions for a reasonable amount of money and for the possibility of a self-sustaining future.

wanted: great south african mysteries

I stumbled across the issue of fly ash over a lunch table in Kempton Park.

'I hear the Indians make bricks out of ash,' a businessman said. 'We've got millions of tons of the stuff lying around the power stations. There must be good business in it.'

Mildly intrigued, I searched the Internet for 'fly ash', found out about Indian low-cost housing and oyster growing, and was hooked. I had discovered, quite by chance, a great South African mystery. There are many more mysteries created by the secretive society we were and the synchronicity of our re-entry into the world as that world enters a new age.

What are these mysteries? Discovering them is a start to unravelling them, and so the first thing to develop is a questioning culture. In Japan, many companies adopt the technique of 'the five times why'. As my geography teacher used to say, 'why' is the most important word an inquiring mind can learn. By asking it five times when anything is not right, you will discover the reasons behind the reasons. It probes the heart of a mystery. A machine could repeatedly break down due to a conflict between two unions. There may never be fresh milk for tea because the directors believe employees should feel grateful for their jobs.

There has never been a black African heavyweight boxing champion of the world. A low-cost, reliable car made for Africa does not exist. In our dry land, we have fine looking sanitaryware that wastes 20 per cent of the water we use. This year, 25 million tons of fly ash will be added to dumps and dams around South Africa. Start 'the five times why' and you can conclude with chrysanthemums in Japan. Which is an appropriate place to be taken by a flower of Eastern thought.

Do not forget the plum,
blooming in
the thicket

Haiku by BASHO, 1644-94

twenty
the third world war

Villages of death

Pearl walks into the village of her birth carrying the collapsible cardboard coffin she bought at the side of the road. She has AIDS and has come home to die. There are no children playing in the street, no men sitting outside, no women in the fields or cattle in the kraal. Because Pearl has come home to one of the South African 'villages of death', decimated by the AIDS virus. As she sees the empty huts her sadness is tempered by a practical thought; at least she has somewhere to sleep tonight.

AIDS world digest, June 2003

We pass on to our children an abused world. Sex is life-threatening, the rain is laced with acid and the sun causes cancer. Private homes and public streets are killing grounds. The best things in life used to be free – now they are deadly.

Over 33 million people around the world are living with HIV/AIDS; over 22 million are in Africa. In North America, 750 000 people are HIV positive. In South Africa, there are 3,2 million; over four times as many, mostly in the early stages of the disease. Every day, 1 500 more South Africans become infected; that is one in 10 of the world's new infections. Because of AIDS, life expectancy in South Africa is predicted to fall from 60 to 40 years by 2010.

AIDS kills heterosexuals and homosexuals, the promiscuous and the faithful, parents and babies. It will kill more people than both world wars. To combat it, we need the Third World War Alliance.

the human cost

Three years ago, when I wrote the first edition of this book, I used this model by Peter Doyle of Metropolitan Life. At the time it seemed to me quite shocking. Now it is regarded as conservative.

	1991	1995	2000	2005
HIV-Infected				
Scenario A*	97 000	970 000	4 112 000	6 410 000
Scenario B*	97 000	970 000	3 700 000	4 762 000
AIDS Sick				
Scenario A	1 190	25 000	259 000	743 000
Scenario B	1 190	25 000	255 000	618 000
AIDS Deaths				
Scenario A	1 350	23 000	203 000	525 000
Scenario B	1 350	23 000	197 000	429 000
Cumulative Deaths				
Scenario A	2 200	47 000	602 002	588 000
Scenario B	2 200	47 000	594 002	321 000

* Scenario A: *'No change in behaviour patterns.'*

* Scenario B: *'Significant changes in sexual behaviour occurring over 12 years into the epidemic.'*

Over 90 per cent of the victims are in two age-groups: 20- to 40-year-olds, who make up 70 per cent or more, and nought to four-year-olds, who constitute 20 per cent. Aids kills men and women starting out in new careers as well as their new-born babies. The future is dying.

When the breadwinner is infected, the family is stunned by a double financial blow. Income is lost and medical expenses escalate. Even existing on basics, families fail to cope and soon exhaust lines of credit. As parents grow ill, children go to live with grandparents, dislocating their education and lives.

In rural areas, labour lost through illness and death will affect food production. Less food leads to poor nutrition, which leads to further illness. In this descending spiral of sickness and hunger, the fragile social compact will self-destruct.

In the cities, our small base of skilled workers and supervisors will be decimated. If they are replaced by a relatively untrained workforce, we can expect industries such as mining to become far more accident prone, while output and productivity will collapse. In the South African National Defence Force it is estimated that 40% of those who serve are HIV positive. How can we protect a country and sub-continent if we cannot protect ourselves?

The epidemic is growing fastest amongst the poor and unemployed, who have no medical aid or financial reserves. The state will have to finance treatment. An already fragile economy could buckle under the strain.

	1991	2000
Direct costs (medical etc)	R94 million*	R7,4 billion
Direct + Indirect costs (including lost production)	R 390 million	R 16,7 billion

* *These figures are based on the average of Doyle's A and B scenarios. In American projections, indirect costs are far higher in comparison with direct costs due to their higher level of employment and earnings.*

If the present trend continues, by 2004 AIDS will account for as much as three-quarters of South Africa's health-care expenditure. If you have AIDS and are homeless, the best place for you is in prison. Compounding the urban nightmare will be AIDS gangs, consisting of the young, poor, angry and dying with nothing left to lose. The police, prison and public health systems will not be able to cope. The cost of private health care will escalate. Other illnesses will not be given the attention they deserve. And criminality will be totally out of control. AIDS affects us all.

the allies of aids

Television and the movies fill impressionable minds with the excitement of sex and violence. In 'adland', if the guy wants the girl, all he has to do is drink, smoke, drive a fast car and use the right deodorant. Sex sells, and to hell with the consequences. The only way to catch AIDS is in AIDS commercials.

The migrant worker system encourages the spread of the disease. Away from his wife and family, a worker combats loneliness and frustration with casual sex. Then he goes home, carrying death amongst his many gifts. As the roads of southern Africa open up, AIDS travels along them. No community, however remote, is untouched. Now, as the Maputo corridor develops, those who travel it call the route 'the highway of death'.

In the cities, the man-about-town sports his concubine at soccer matches while his wife cleans the church. Monogamy in Africa is not a cultural imperative.

In townships, a 15-year-old daughter may bring food home for the family and no questions are asked. Or the wife has found another man who can provide. Street children at the age of seven sell their bodies for glue to sniff.

The other allies of AIDS are those who say it is not really happening, that it is a blessing in disguise, and that TB, cancer and road fatalities cost South Africa more. AIDS quietly destroys any chance of an African renaissance, while we debate the issue.

ignorance, poverty, and myths

Ignorance: Many South Africans, especially those who are most at risk, still do not know what AIDS is or how to prevent it.

Poverty: No work; no money; no prospects and living in overcrowded shack settlements where sex and crime are the only pastimes.

renaissance dawning

Myths: Women are second-class citizens, condoms are the white man's way of stopping blacks having babies, and raping a 10-year-old cures AIDS.

'AIDS is nothing new for all African tribes. You can lay a snare for somebody through your girlfriend or wife. If a man messes with her, he gets a disease. His balls will swell up, or he will be eaten away. He can sit in the sun and the whole time he will be feeling cold. If he does not own up, he will die. He must go back to that family and tell them he slept with the wife.

'Then he must get the wee-wee of that woman. He must drink it with other herbs. It is like a vaccination. Wee-wee helps your immune system. It builds up resistance in your body, like a virus after a snake-bite.

'Now the problem is that you have HIV for years before you get AIDS. We can deal with any emergencies that come up, as long as you know where you got it. If it was 10 years ago, you don't know where you got it. So you cannot know what woman's wee-wee to drink.' JOHNNY N

'We know we can cure cancer, and now we are curing AIDS.' TRADITIONAL HEALER

AIDS education is failing in South Africa despite the efforts of many dedicated individuals. There is no national, home-grown strategy. American solutions don't work here.

Nearly one out of 10 South Africans is HIV positive. One in three of sexually active adults in KwaZulu-Natal is infected. How many AIDS patients can our continent take before it collapses into anarchy? If the march of the disease cannot be stopped in South Africa, the sub-continent will become like a huge leper colony, shunned by the world. Tourists and business will stay away.

South Africa has an AIDS advertising budget, but more is spent on advertising a single brand of cigarettes. Think of the billboards you see on the highways and in town. How many of them say 'Wear a condom'?

And advertising can never do the job of education. There are articles, TV programmes and radio chat shows. They count for less than a week of *Egoli* viewership. Like everyone else, we prefer soap operas to lectures. In schools, AIDS is still a new subject and the figures say it isn't being learnt.

In the protected suburbs it is still unusual to know someone dying of AIDS. It has not touched us, and there seem to be so many more vital issues. The politicians have other things on their minds and big business would rather be associated with football, golf, education – anything but AIDS. The war is being lost without a fight.

the war-chest

To fight a war you need money. But don't expect it all to come from the government.

Housing, education, job creation, water and electricity are all important and urgent. AIDS is important, and the government have it on their list, but dying in five years time does not command the same urgency as being homeless and jobless. It is not first on the politicians' agenda.

All the more reason for South African industry to prioritise it. An AIDS-stricken nation will not produce as much gold or food, it will not buy as many motor cars, clothes or soft drinks. The boom in the economy will never happen and the focus of global investors will move elsewhere.

How does industry fill the war-chest? Who pays, and how much? Which is the simplest method? What costs the least to collect?

For a start, consider the nation's advertisers. The ad industry spends R55 billion on advertising and sponsorship. Take one per cent of that communication money and use it for an AIDS education fund. The South African Advertising Research Foundation imposes a levy of 0,5 per cent to collect facts and figures about the market. A one per cent AIDS levy to protect this market does not seem excessive.

Fifty-five million rand a year can be collected relatively easily and inexpensively. Media buyers can pledge to be one per cent more effective, and so the real cost will shrink. The public will know who sponsored the education fund – excellent public relations for the advertising industry.

'Why pick on us?' soap makers and supermarkets may complain. 'Pick on the industrial giants who aren't big advertising spenders.'

And while everyone debates who goes first, there is no one to fight the enemy. Alternatively, the association of advertisers could take the moral high ground. The opportunity to save a subcontinent doesn't happen every day.

Assuming there is an extra R55 million in the kitty, what should it be used for?

sex in the classroom

AIDS and sex education must become a major school subject. People will protest because smut is brought into the classroom, condoms are not approved by their church and we cannot expose our innocent children to such terrible things.

Reason with them. It is far better for a child to pass an AIDS exam than fail an AIDS test.

The annual R55 million advertiser's fund will pay for AIDS teaching materials, as well as teaching the teachers. Education cannot stop unprotected sex, but it can dispel myths and clarify the options. When sex education becomes a matric subject, knowing about AIDS will be a necessary precondition for further education and a good job.

> Yesterday, Terri couldn't come to see us. She was in hospital again. So three of us in the class were chosen to go and see her. She looked very thin and pale. We could see she was tired, and the blotches on her skin were bigger. But she smiled as we approached the bed.
>
> 'Sit down', she said, 'and bring out your notebooks. This is your next AIDS lesson.'
>
> Extract of a school essay, 2003

Reality enhances the learning process. Dying AIDS patients will serve society, and find meaning in their own tragedy by saving the young. The corporations that are not big advertisers can make their own contribution by sponsoring 10, 50, or 100 people with AIDS to spread the message.

> 'I am a married schoolteacher and I am HIV-positive. I knew my husband had

other women but I did not dare ask him to wear a condom. Now I will die from my embarrassment.' VERA N

People with AIDS do not have all the answers, but they can help us ask the right questions.

sex and the bottom line

Public companies have a public duty to inform stakeholders about their AIDS policies and programmes. These should be given prominence in their annual reports. How effective is their awareness training? How are they helping behavioural change? If these companies use sexual allure in their advertising and promotion, how do they achieve a balanced morality?

When employees are tested HIV-positive, will they receive counselling and treatment? Workers who develop AIDS make financial demands on their employers. How will these demands be met? Some corporations have meticulous AIDS policies, drawn up in consultation with the unions. Many others are heading for crisis management.

The AIDS section of an annual report will be another measure for investors and analysts.

spreading the message

Adults not working for big corporations can receive AIDS education from another source, the traditional healer. More than 80 per cent of black South Africans use the services of inyangas and sangomas. There are between 150 000 and 400 000 traditional healers in the country, who belong to over 100 associations. Yet KwaZulu-Natal is the only province that recognises these healers, and few medical-aid schemes accept them.

Some healers are charlatans who claim to cure any disease, bring the dead back to life, and cause others to fall ill or die. They are dangerous in the AIDS battle as patients take a threat less seriously when they are assured of a simple cure.

True traditional healers have a deep knowledge of natural remedies and communicate well with their patients. They must be enlisted as soldiers in the AIDS war, teaching every patient the realities of the disease and how it can be prevented. The inyangas and sangomas can show people how to use condoms and distribute them. Rural people trust a sangoma before a government health official, and there are many more to spread the message.

Inyangas and sangomas want to play an official part in the health system of this country. They believe companies should allow their patients sick leave when they recommend it, and that medical-aid societies must view traditional healers and doctors as equals. Helping the war against AIDS will give inyangas and sangomas recognition and respect. Doctors and AIDS workers can hold classes at regional sangoma headquarters, and the lessons will flow out to those who are most threatened and difficult to reach.

At the same time, we need all those in the public eye to speak out against the disease. A few years ago, Uganda made prevention of AIDS a national priority, the responsibility of all its role models. Every time a leader, from President Yoweri Museveni down, appears in public, mention is made of the pandemic and the need to wear condoms. Non-government organisations (NGOs) are encouraged to cut through bureaucracy and prejudice in their efforts to fight the disease. This strategy has enabled Uganda to reverse its infection rate, the only country in Africa to do so.

In South Africa, there seems to be too much else on the agenda. Violent crime, corruption, unemployment, housing, affirmative action, truth and reconciliation are all more speechworthy. National leaders must set the tone and strategy, but this war will be won or lost in the community trenches. The tragedy of the *Sarafina* debacle is that the government got involved with the tactics. The money wasted on one grandiose production could have funded hundreds of community-based initiatives. I have seen one, a musical created and produced by a group in an East Rand township and performed in a converted meeting room, that left everyone in tears. Communities against AIDS will ensure that appropriate messages are continuously sounded at weddings, funerals, musical events and political rallies. Cultural norms have to be overturned; the core message must be repeated and repeated.

southern comfort

What alternatives to unprotected sex can be offered to the millions of southern Africans who cannot afford any other kind of entertainment? AIDS is rampant in the Red Cross refugee camps of Malawi. When you have lost your home, job and money, and when you are crowded together in makeshift shacks where malnutrition and disease run riot, will you listen to anyone who says you should make love with a condom?

Migrant workers will not spend seven nights a week drinking and watching television. Long-distance truck drivers will not go to bed every night with a good book, and the man-about-town will not suddenly embrace monogamy.

The world's oldest profession is now the world's most dangerous. Some prostitutes have reacted by charging customers two prices; you pay the lower rate if you wear a condom. If prostitution is allowed and controlled, it would become safer. The Prostitutes' Charter would restrict sex for sale to agreed red light areas. Prostitutes swear to make sure a condom is always used, and consent to regular testing to check they are drug- and AIDS-free. If they keep to their side of the bargain and pay tax, they will be legal and unharassed. But if they break the charter, they go to jail.

Controlling prostitution helps. But to defeat AIDS, virginity must once again be prized. There is a ritual that calls for unmarried girls to be regularly examined by an older woman of the village to see if they are still virgins. The girls walk to a running stream, each carrying a clay pot. If her seal is unbroken, she fills the pot with water and takes it to her father. Otherwise, she may only fill the pot half-way, and her father sees the young man responsible. The filled pot is a traditional sign of family pride and honour. It can become a modern symbol of personal values and health.

Another custom was aimed at making boys who reach puberty more manageable. A specially chosen old lady of the village has a stick with small knobs on the side. She inserts this stick into each boy's rectum. This is where, she tells him, all his sex nerves are. Then she twists the stick around. For a time the boy doesn't think about girls. When his thoughts turn that way again, the lady with her stick is ready.

Is there a less painful way of getting the message across? Honouring virginity has been a part of African society. An alliance of traditional and modern leaders can make the old ways relevant again. The women of Africa are the most harmed by AIDS. As they slowly emerge from centuries of discrimination, and as they begin to control their lives and reproduction, they will be the frontline soldiers in the Third World War.

looking after the sick

If we do everything right, we can stop AIDS becoming an epidemic. But we will not wipe it out. AIDS will be endemic in South Africa within ten years, killing over half a million men, women and children a year. We will see in this country the 'villages of death' that have spread like a plague throughout sub-Saharan Africa.

How will the state, community and family care for all the dying? Will we have AIDS colonies in rural areas shunned by the rest of us? Or can AIDS centres help sufferers become vital members of society?

Will only the wealthy few receive expensive, life-extending drugs? How will families of AIDS victims escape onerous debt? An alliance between the medical profession, social workers and traditional healers will be needed to counsel the sick and their families; people with AIDS should help their fellow sufferers; corporates must match compassion with commercial reality; all those that have the time and will to do something for society must be mobilised.

We can pray that a low-cost vaccine is discovered somewhere in the world. Meanwhile, we must fight the AIDS war with all the resources we can put together. If we lose, this land cannot fulfil its promise. Africa will be purgatory, and the world will turn away.

twenty-one
educere: to draw out

The Mandela sandwich

'You know the best thing that happened for us kids right after the '94 elections? The old man gave us a sandwich every day.' South Africa's newest million-rand rugby player smiles as I open the farm gates and we drive on.

'The Mandela sandwich kept me going to school. I was always hungry, and the feeding-scheme aunty gave us two thick pieces of brown bread with meatpaste in it every morning at eleven.'

We slow down at a row of outbuildings. 'This is my school,' Philly 'Hands' Skosana says with quiet pride. 'And here is the field where I learnt my sport.' We walk over to it as the schoolbell rings and 175 children pour out of the classrooms and race across to greet their greatest hero, the Duikerfontein Farm School boy who plays for the Blue Bulls.

Philly Skosana comes back each month to teach rugby and tell kids to stay at school as long as they can. While he coaches them on the line-out, I am taken around the classrooms by the headmaster. 'Things have got better in the last 10 years,' he tells me. 'We now have water, the roof doesn't leak, and we have Hands. He shows us all that school is the path to success.'

The headmaster gave Hands his name. Philly started as a wing three-quarter because he ran like the wind. But he kept dropping the ball. Each time he did so, the headmaster would wave his old cowhide sjambok and shout: 'Hands, boy, hands!'. The headmaster coached Philly after hours, while the boy watched the cattle, throwing him the rugby ball as he swerved around another munching cow. 'Hands, boy, hands!'

His speed, agility and eventually safe hands have taken Skosana to a two-year contract with the Blue Bulls that guarantees him R1 million a year. If they do well in the Currie Cup and Super 12, he doubles his earnings. That's before the corporate world throws a treasure-chest of sponsorships his way.

Hands t-shirts are in the flea-markets. Hands cups, sunglasses and rugby boots are in production. The 21-year-old player is unaffected by the sudden limelight.

'I've been lucky', Philly says. 'I will be a millionaire doing what I love. But without the Mandela sandwich, who knows? I may not have been worth ten cents.'

The rugby ball is tossed from boy to boy. When it is dropped, the chorus rings 'Hands, Hands' around the pitch.

Of the 20 million children in South Africa, nine million live in poverty-stricken households. And millions do not have the comfort of a family. There are over 15 000 street-children in Gauteng alone. Most do not roam the streets by choice. One comes from Tugela Ferry to Hillbrow looking for his mother; another leaves home because his new step-father beat him; a third is sent by her drunken parents to find money any way she can. Some street-children find their way to hostels and makeshift schools. One school was temporarily housed in the Braamfontein YMCA in June 1995. There were 119 children in need of special attention and love; only two were girls. The rest rarely make it to the shelters because the street absorbs them. They are used as prostitutes from the age of six, until drugs, sex and violence kills them.

These street-children now have a school in Mayfair. They dream of being doctors, drivers, electricians, lawyers and policemen. What they would like now is a proper uniform and a schoolcase; to be like other children. They invent a name for their school. The old Mayfair Primary is now the New Nation School.

In a farm school less than an hour from Johannesburg's northern suburbs, the biggest problem for 175 pupils and four teachers is water.

educere: to draw out

There is a tap in the next field, but the borehole has been dry for years. A local contractor said it could cost R50 000 for a new borehole. It may as well be R100 million.

There is a classroom that remains half-built. The children freeze and bake from season to season under an unprotected tin roof. There are holes in the walls, and one day perhaps they will be able to replace the washed-out, peeling, 20-year-old posters. Neither the school nor the headmaster has a phone, so communication is slow, and when he reports to the district superintendent, he must conduct his business in the backyard. Two of the four teachers hitch lifts to school. They arrive late or not at all. The children range from six to 20 years old, and most who get to standard five, pass. But it is not easy. When they leave school for the day, tending to the cattle, cleaning the home, and caring for young siblings all take the place of homework.

In rural Africa children represent wealth. They are the labour force that look after parents in their old age, and so the more children you have, the better. A morning of school and an afternoon of cattle-tending is seen as fair; why hire casual labour when you have a large family?

The feeding scheme that gives every child milk and a Mandela sandwich each day brings many more hungry young ones to school. Education promises them a better life. Many rural parents are only partly convinced; they will forego child labour once they see economic benefits. Reading and writing are not enough. Educated children must get work, because if education doesn't put more food on the table, of what use is it? We must estimate what kind of jobs will exist for the next 20 years, before we can know what to teach children today.

Based on a growing consensus of views, I see four broad categories of growth for employment in South Africa. Each category relates to an ability that can be recognised and nurtured early in life. They are:

- Carers

- Builders

- Entrepreneurs

- Entertainers.

the commerce of caring

If South Africa Inc. travels the high road, the fastest growing industry creating the most jobs, especially in rural areas, will be tourism. Our children should know how to be tourist- and environment-carers. They can be shown the southern African traditions of courtesy and sharing with strangers. They will learn how these traditions help everyone to prosper, the options tourists have around the world, how vital it is to give them a quality experience, the difference between service and servility, and how an unspoiled environment is a paying proposition. The students will go on field trips, mostly close to home but some further afield, supplementing classroom skills with practical knowledge of their area and experience in dealing with people. These field trips, urban as well as rural, could bring in revenue for the school and pupils. (For instance, a shopping mall could 'employ' a school-class of carers over the Christmas period to direct shoppers and help carry bags to their cars.)

As well as tourist-care, health care for the sick and aged will remain a human intensive industry. Valuing people may become this country's global advantage. We who did it worst have the capability of doing it best. While Japanese students chant in unison the co-ordinates of a turning-point of the parabola, South African students can discover the inner satisfaction that comes from helping others. A caring culture that starts in nursery school will help this nation's healing process and prepare the young for more job opportunities than any other industry offers.

builders of the new south africa

There are builders of houses, dams and cyberhighways. South Africa needs them all.

One million low-cost homes are urgently required, as are 50 000 more classrooms. Hotels, convention centres and exclusive hideaways are appearing from Cape Town to the Okavango. Townships begin to enjoy their own shopping malls and clinics. Over the next 15 years, road, rail, port and pipeline projects will open a flow of trade through the subcontinent.

educere: to draw out

To make and maintain the new southern Africa we need bricklayers, roadmakers, electricians, architects, town planners and project managers. Students that show an early aptitude can start by building their own classrooms, under the supervision of local and national builders.

We also need new ideas. Technological advances and knowledge growth create national wealth. In South Africa there are only 17 000 engineers and scientists per million people. The ratio is three times higher in Europe and over six times higher in the United States. If we narrow the South Africa to Europe ratio to 1:2 within 10 years, we need to create 500 000 new engineers and scientists. Meanwhile, school laboratories that were burnt down in 1976 are still in ruins. For science to reach out to the underprivileged, sets of experiments should be made available for any young enquiring mind. Other countries offer a laboratory-in-a-box to schools that cannot afford a full-blown laboratory. These mini-labs contain a whole range of experiments and scientific activities and can be stored in a broom cupboard when not in use. Perhaps a corporate sponsor might find donating mini scientific labs to 1 000 schools more powerful for the brand, and more uplifting for the country than another TV ad or sports sponsorship.

Building faster cyberhighways, creating on-line communities and effective e-commerce models will be tickets to employability anywhere in the world and vital for South Africa if we want a sizeable stake in the Internet economy. As Americans become a minority on the Internet, other clusters of IT excellence are developing. Tel Aviv is the hub of Israel's booming hi-tech industry; the sector is growing 2,5 times faster than the rest of the economy, employing highly-skilled, well-rewarded labour.

The emergence of Tel Aviv is no accident. It is a hi-tech incubator where entrepreneurs can find infrastructure, seed capital, research and advice. This incubator principle is now being applied in the Western Cape. The Capricorn Science and Manufacturing Park, near Muizenberg, is expected to generate 40 000 jobs. The size of seven Sandton Cities, Capricorn will focus on hi-tech and communications, combining six-year tax holidays with an environment created around a lake on the edge of the Indian Ocean. But initiatives like Capricorn will never fulfil their potential until the region supplies sufficient skilled labour.

Cape Town's Gateway Discovery Trust has been taking science and hi-tech to schools since 1991. As a part of its outreach programme, the Discovery Mobile, a bus fitted out with an interactive science exhibition, travels to the underfunded primary schools of the Western Cape. It is a worthy start, but two hours of wonder is soon eclipsed by the realities of poverty. If the shareholders of Capricorn Park devote a percentage of their revenues to providing computers and educational software to schools in the neighbouring Cape Flats, they would be providing for their own future.

incubating entrepreneurs

On average, our labour force increases by 476 000 people each year. We already have an unemployment rate of 40 per cent. Increasing efficiencies does not mean that existing companies in the formal sector will be significant new employers. South Africa needs to create hundreds of thousands of entrepreneurs before it offers, in the medium- and long-term, millions of new, sustainable jobs. This indicates that schools must teach entrepreneurship as a core subject. As there are IQ tests, so there are entrepreneur tests for children, and international figures suggest that one child in seven has potential.

Entrepreneur training in South Africa has been pioneered by Richards Bay Minerals. It is called EASE (Entrepreneurship and Self-Employment) and is available to anyone with the resources to teach it as a year school subject, or six-week full-time course. Teachers are given free training. An adapted Zulu version – Basic Entrepreneurship Education Programme (BEEP) – has been introduced for use at skills training centres and for marginalised youth. Early victories range from children who employ their parents in such diverse activities as cake-making and web-page design, to the young lad who rented his mother's cell-phone, took orders for pizza in the school playground, then ordered them wholesale from his local pizza parlour.

Universities around the world are beginning to recognise that entrepreneurialism is a legitimate subject; recently the London School of Economics added an entrepreneurial chair to its distinguished roster. In South Africa, we will fast-track successful entrepreneurs by creating

educere: to draw out

a selection and learning process that flows from primary school to post-graduate studies. We also need inner city colleges that attract those who show entrepreneurial rather than academic ability.

young entertainers for an aging world

As hijackers and drug barons monopolise the headlines, showing a seemingly easy and glamourous escape from the ghetto, South Africa cries out for more young role models and heroes. Sports and entertainment can provide – and you do not have to wait until you are 50 to reach the top. The aging world, especially men, love watching sport. As they enter their mellow years, they gladly pay for a non-stop offering. Most sports will have their round-the-clock TV stations. In the United States you can already tune in to the angler channel and watch, with hypnotic fascination, a man standing in a cold river failing to catch anything for three hours. Sport is big business; the stars are paid millions and television deals have entered the billions. The search is on for the best global talent and South Africa has a large pool of potentials.

Boxing is a wealth- and hero-maker, and is relatively inexpensive to teach in schools. One South African world champion learnt his craft in a Zululand pit, into which a few dozen village boys were thrown with their fighting sticks. Whoever still stood at the end was the winner. In America, a more conventional route to boxing glory is the Golden Gloves Tournament. It starts in small towns each year and ends by celebrating a full house of champions. In South Africa, young talent is often overlooked or ruined in mismatched prize-fights. Our own Golden Gloves, sponsored by the likes of Gillette or Lion Lager, could create an Olympic champion or two and perhaps the first black South African heavyweight champion of the world.

A team sport is a more efficient use of young male energy, and rugby is the best way, a teacher told me, that one adult can keep 30 high-spirited boys out of mischief for the best part of an hour and a half. Team for team, it offers 40 per cent more employment than football. South Africa has world-class facilities and coaches, as well as well-heeled owners and supporters. All we need is a continuing supply of players with raw ability. The demographics dictate a new strategy.

For each white baby in South Africa there are 12 black babies. There are more coloured than white children under 13 years old. Unless the sport takes root in farm schools, shack settlements and townships, the glorious South African rugby tradition will fade.

Football has a massive, committed following in South Africa and as African stars make their mark in Europe, thousands of local hopefuls lace up to take their place. Cricket has become more TV-friendly and offers longer-term employment than the physical winter sports. Basketball can be the next major South African sporting industry. It is an ideal team activity in the heart of a concrete jungle; the equipment and clothes look cool and the superheroes are mostly black.

All sports promote health, discipline and reduction in crime; as the government White Paper says: 'A child in sport is a child out of court'. The first priority is to encourage more children and adults to play. We regard ourselves as a sporting nation, yet less than 30 per cent of South Africans regularly play any sport, opposed to nearly 90 per cent of Australians. It is hardly surprising when a township of 100 000 has a single dusty soccer pitch, and physical education at most black schools has been allowed to collapse.

The White Paper emphasises the need to grow a sporting culture from grassroots. Sponsorships by major corporations will offer cricket bats and rugby balls to farm schools, as well as large cheques and cups to national heroes. Teachers will be incentivised to take sport seriously. Discovering young sporting stars will become as important as developing mathematicians. Train-the-trainer programmes spread knowledge and enthusiasm. Paid talent scouts will roam the clubs and schools of each province, alerted by enthusiastic teachers, local newspaper reports and community comment. Scholarships for underprivileged sporting stars to attend the best endowed schools can be funded by national and local authorities. Affirmative selection starts here.

Additional funding can come from a South African equivalent of the British football pools. An investment in sport is an investment in youth, health and future prosperity.

Like sport, the entertainment industry relies on talent more than academic excellence; it is a significant net employer and thrives on youth, creating many young role-models, often from disadvantaged backgrounds.

South Africa is experiencing a surge of interest in local music, from kwaito to traditional choirs. New venues are opening for live performances, prime-time TV features the best of African music videos and new radio stations are showcases for indigenous talent. Home-grown acts are increasing in confidence. Rap music has its roots in Africa, and the new street-poets are sharing authentic experiences over an African beat rather than copying American ghetto life. New technology reduces costs, allowing a South African group to be produced on-line by a Los Angeles or London hit wizard.

A growing local middle class is buying hi-fis for home and car. Music Business International forecasts that South African album sales will grow to $530 million in the year 2000; an almost fourfold increase in five years. If local artists enjoy 60 per cent of the sales, their contribution will rise from $76 million to $336 million. That excludes sales in Africa and abroad as well money made from live shows, jingles, movie scores, TV themes and advertising endorsements. This robust domestic market has the opportunity to breed acts, even musical styles, that aurally refresh and excite a jaded world.

Kilimanjaro on top

Kilimanjaro is on top of the world! Their second album, 'Warrior Dance', has cracked the number one spot in the world's biggest three markets: America, Japan and Germany. The pan-African group consists of a Zulu male choir, a Shangaan guitarist, Mbqanga fretless bass, Burundi drummers and sampled African horns.

Music International, October 2004

Another growth industry will be television programming. As electricity becomes increasingly available, millions of new viewers from Cape Town to Cairo will tune in each year. South Africa has the facilities and the infrastructure to create an annual 10 000 hours of TV programmes for this country, as well as content for the African continent. There will be joint productions, dubbing facilities for 50 official languages, and chances to create an Afrocentric CNN, *The Bold and the Beautiful*, *60 Minutes*, and *Cosby Show*.

The local industry will need writers who crystallise our lives here. Writers who should be discovered and nurtured whilst still at school, learning to speak with their own voices, not those borrowed from other lands and cultures. There will be jobs for actors, newsreaders, producers, technicians, make-up artists and moguls – as well as more musicians. As this infrastructure develops, the Highveld could become the new Hollywood, with a hi-tech new millennium network of studios where rents are low and the sun shines almost all the time.

African art has a vibrant reality and affordability that is a welcome change from the minimalist, highly-priced abstractions of Western offerings. With more international exposure, it can spread to the boardrooms and homes of Europe and America. African design is being used in clothing, jewellery and houseware. The black diaspora and a nation proud of its roots can push Afrocentricity onto the world stage. The movement will grow if it is fed and schools are the ideal feeding-places. We must educate our children to see the world through African eyes.

earn while you learn

If schools are a practice ground for the rest of your life, some practical experiments in how to earn money would be useful. Trainee builders could assist with a community project, charging a school rate that allows a créche, a new classroom or a market to be built. The entertainers can hold a sports and culture day, with young entrepreneurs swelling school coffers with the sale of programmes, pieces of art, and a modest bookmaking operation based on the sports results.

Most of our youth will leave school for the university of hard knocks; in the foreseeable future, they will be poor and jobless. It is time to reconsider the pre-industrial age apprentice system. Young apprentices are expected to be hard-working, uncomplaining and low paid. They are learning their trade. After their apprenticeship, they leave their employer-teacher unless invited to stay and then an employment contract is drawn up. Low pay means an employer can afford the apprentice as well as the time to train. For the young and unemployed as well as the community, a few hundred rands a month and an opportunity is better than empty days and the ebb of hope.

educere: to draw out

Education comes from the Latin word, *educere*, meaning 'to draw out'. Yet our obsession with doing well in exams leads us to making education a 'shoving-in' process. Each child has a unique gift; if teachers recognise and nurture it, they become true educators.

Maria Montessori was fascinated by the ability of young children to concentrate on tasks they choose for themselves. They have a natural curiosity and a desire to learn. She created a set of learning materials that are self-correcting. Through their repeated use, children can experience and learn for themselves. For instance, by arranging Montessori beads in rows, squares and cubes, a child becomes intuitively numerate. Each day, a child chooses the materials she wants to work with, while the teacher is an observer and guide. In Montessori schools, children from three to six years old are in the same classroom, as are children from seven to nine, and 10 to 12, developing at the pace most comfortable for each, finding activities they enjoy and do best.

If Maria Montessori was in an African farm school today, rather than in Italy 75 years ago, she may have devised different materials, but her principles are validated by current realities. Pupils of many different ages learn together in the same class. The size of the classes means that the question-and-response method involves only a few. Self-teaching materials give each pupil a unique learning path. And if these materials could be made in rural communities, using local materials, education will be creating employment where it is needed most.

And if Maria Montessori was in California, she would probably be a software programmer creating multi-activity CD-ROMs. I work on a computer from home as does my wife and our five-year-old son Daniel. He has a selection of educational CD-ROMs that he plays when he wants to (within reason). Digital education is fun, challenging and personalised. As many children as possible must be given access to computers and good educational software. When more South African schoolchildren become digitally enabled, it will be worthwhile to produce CDs with a local flavour. One of Daniel's favourites is 'Putt-Putt saves the Zoo', an animated interactive adventure that features a perky little car on a mission to rescue some lost animals. With local production (and sponsorship) we could have titles like 'Citi saves the Kruger'.

If we combine Montessori-Africa with Montessori-California, then encourage the values of collaborative effort through shared projects, music and sport, we will give our children a high-touch and hi-tech education. Teachers will be discoverers and guides, drawing out the best that each child can do.

> 'Infant mortality rates rank South Africa amongst the 35 worst countries in the world. Without urgent effort, thousands more infants will die, thousands more who survive will be stunted and many more will suffer the violence and stress which poverty engenders.'
> National Institute for Economic Policy, 1995

> 'Young people are our country's most important resource.'
> RDP White Paper

twenty-two
the women of Africa

The men sat by the fire and their brains were inert, as their blood flowed heavy with the accumulation from the living day.

The women were different. On them too was the drowse of blood-intimacy, calves sucking and hens running together in droves, and young geese palpitating in the hand while the food was pushed down their throttle. But the women looked out from the heated, blind intercourse of farm-life, to the spoken world beyond. They were aware of the lips and the mind of the world speaking and giving utterance, they heard the sound in the distance and they strained to listen.

DH LAWRENCE, The Rainbow

I asked Richard Cornwell, then director of current affairs at the Africa Institute, which single thing could lift Africa out of the mess the continent is in; what should be our focus? First he said, re-create the network of trading stores that war and apartheid had demolished. But the answer did not seem to satisfy him, for then he said he would have to think about it and would phone me.

The next morning my answering machine buzzed with his excitement. I made a mental list of what he was most likely to tell me, and called him back. His new answer wasn't on my list. He told me Africa had to emancipate the women, and then women would emancipate Africa.

Emancipation goes far deeper than passing laws, although the laws are an essential first step. This is the best of times for women's emancipation in Africa, and it is the worst of times. Men are under threat more than ever before. The economically empowered woman is a family necessity and threat. The numbers of women in business are increasing, but the fastest growing business open to them is the sale of sex.

The women of Africa must progress from being a reproductive vehicle to being a productive source. The poor have too many mouths to feed. There is a proven relationship between female education and a lower birthrate. As young girls learn that their options are far greater than their dependence on men and child labour, they take control of their own reproductive abilities and lives.

Yet across Africa, the school enrolment rate for girls is falling. The benefits of education are seen as curses by many parents. Schoolgirls come home with ideas that threaten the family structure. Daughters are considered the primary source of unpaid labour. Others are part of a gruesome new trade. The increase in AIDS awareness has led to child prostitutes being favoured, as their customers believe they are less likely to be infected.

The rural areas of Africa remain untouched by gender equality laws passed in remote parliaments. The injustices and pain go deeper than a banker refusing a loan without the husband's permission, even though a woman is statistically a far smaller risk than a man. In Tanzania, a woman who dies unmarried is buried right at the edge of her father's land. Tradition demands she has no claim to it, in life or death. A boy's birth is a time of feasting. When a girl is born, no beast is slaughtered.

When the boy grows up, he counts his wealth in terms of cattle and wives. Parents of girls pray the rich young man will pay a good *lobola* (cash, please) and give her a better home. There are others in the production line to work and cook.

There are also more women in positions of power than ever before in Africa. And their number is increasing rapidly. In one election alone, South Africa came from near the bottom to be ranked seventh in the world for women in parliament. Big business still drags its feet, but the informal sector is a different story. If one out of seven hawkers is a potential entrepreneur, the economy is about to get a long overdue shot of woman power. The question is, can men cope?

the problem with men

In general, men are more aggressive than women. It could be the hormones, growing up with toy guns, playing rugby, hunting for dinosaurs and bringing home the bacon. Men usually start the big trouble, especially when they are in crisis. And around the world, as well as in South Africa, men are in an unprecedented multiple crisis. Since the caveman and his club you knew who a real man was – the breadwinner, head of the household and unquestionably heterosexual. Now, suddenly, everything is changing

Feminism created the burning bra, shelves of feminist literature and real change. Moderate feminists want equal rights, while radicals seek to overturn traditional social structures. When male dominance is questioned, men feel threatened. While anti-feminists retreat into the male laager, pro-feminists seek to redefine the male role.

The New Age man is sensitive, caring, changes the nappies, does the washing up and polishes the kitchen floor. Or does he? In taverns you may hear about a potion women give their men that makes them unmasculine and soft. A man who does woman's work at home is judged to be a victim of this potion, and so real men cannot perform women's duties. No potion is needed for the great white male. Comments at the pub such as 'Who wears the trousers?' and 'She's got you by the balls', are enough to make a closet liberal pledge that a man's place is in front of the TV between the beer and biltong.

Gay liberation has dealt another blow to traditional masculinity. Real men are confused, defensive and vitriolic about the blatant visibility of their homosexual brothers. Gays are ridiculed, abused and beaten up by confused straights who wonder how straight they really are. Only slightly less damaging for the red-blooded male psyche is a gay woman. He and his fellows are being rejected *en masse*. If she is unattractive, things are fine; she couldn't get a real man anyway. But if she is 'hot', 'what a waste'.

Together with these sociological shifts, the woman's orgasm and the birth control pill force men to reassess their sexual supremacy. The vaginal orgasm implies entry must be made, and what better tool of entry than the man's? The clitoral orgasm changes the pleasure paradigm. Entry is no longer nirvana. The male and his tool are among the options.

Since the 1960s, the birth control pill has given women equal opportunity for sexual gratification. Sex with or without babies becomes her choice. AIDS and the condom restrict the power of the pill outside monogamous relationships. But, one on one, the woman has shifted a key responsibility. She, not the man, is in control of reproduction.

The communication revolution has also exposed real men. Television breaks down information ghettos placed around women at home. It takes her behind the scenes. While he talks about a late night at the office, she watches the soap opera and sees the boss making out with the secretary. While he says this is the way life must be, she sees a hundred alternatives. Television in rural Africa will be more of a dramatic revelation than it was in the United States and Europe because the information ghettos have been more enforced here. Television programmes are also far more outspoken now than ever before.

In today's consumerist world, the one-earner family is a rarity. The poor need more than one income to survive. The middle class have to pay for two cars, good schools and overseas holidays. The wealthy equate careers with social acceptance. In the 50 years between 1960 and 2010, the percentage of women in the South African labour force will double to 42 per cent. Manufacturing jobs that need men's strength are quickly disappearing. The ability to tap into a computer network counts far more than the power to wield a pickaxe.

'Mr Middle America' tries to deal with the rights of gays, women and minorities while being 'rightsized' out of a job. Masculinity crisis literature such as Robert Bly's *Iron John*, has groups of men beating drums at weekend retreats. Violence, especially against women, is increasing.

Until now, South Africa has been a last refuge for the real man. He ruled in the home, workplace and government. A woman who titled herself 'Ms' was told by a South African customs official it was not acceptable. She replied it is acceptable everywhere else in the world.

'Everywhere else in the world is not South Africa,' the customs chauvinist warned her. 'Miss, Mrs or stay out!'

The sudden double whammy of racial and sexual affirmative action gives the man's man, especially in the civil service, a new boss who is a black Ms.

The high levels of black urban unemployment mean that many traditional breadwinners sit at home while their wives put food on the table. Often he dares not ask how it got there. Sometimes his teenage daughter will bring money home. He knows that a mouth that asks too many questions will not be fed. He bottles up his humiliation, and sometimes it explodes. A man who loses self-esteem is a dangerous animal to himself, his family and the world.

Of the men who work, many live far from home. Their sons are born and raised in a world of women. Yet, when they are four or five, the boys are tossed out of the sorority. They are not allowed to do housework or play with dolls – that's woman's stuff. Resentment may start here. In the old days, the boy would be apprenticed to his father, following his trade, ethics and habits. Now the father is absent while the mother kicks him out of the nest. Meanwhile, clothes, beer and women tempt the lonely migrant worker and stop money flowing back home to his family. The young, cast-out boy is angry on an empty stomach.

The problem with men is that we are not as tough as we thought we were. Challenges to our authority and virility cause an unwelcome host of mental and physical problems that include stress, depression, alcoholism, drug dependency, violence, sexual deviancy, heart disease and early death. When the going gets tough, men either hit out or give up. Unless someone helps us through.

they should all be exported

Plenty of South African women have had enough of their men; they are spoilt boys who whimper and lash out at the slightest reverse. 'They should all be exported' flashes through Gauteng homes via the airwaves.

The burdens of women in Africa are becoming unbearable. Not only do they have their full plate of injustices, they also must digest the male in crisis. It has been said that France would be wonderful without the French. Now it is said that marriage would be wonderful without men.

Relationships are becoming as meaningful as disposable razors. Poor men are liabilities and rich men must be used. Survival takes what it takes. The more women need men economically, the less they like and respect them. But the less women need men, the more men are threatened. We have reached the racial bottom line before the sexual bottom line, yet the line is the same. In order to survive, we need each other. To grow and thrive, we need to give each other all the support we can. Because women have great inner strength and males are in a multiple crisis, it makes sense that the woman, once again, offers her support first. And the second time and the third time, despite rejections.

There is a Billy Joel song that repeats, 'We didn't start the fire'. Women did not start the Second World War, ethnic cleansing in Bosnia, the multiple Middle East crises, slaughter in Rwanda or hit-squads in South Africa. Women make up over 50 per cent of the population, yet create less than five per cent of the violence. They didn't start the fire, but perhaps they can put it out.

Before women can release themselves from injustice, they must release their men from fear, insecurity and violence. It may not be fair, but then what is?

psychologists and spies

Peter Gabriel wrote a song that he sings with Kate Bush called 'Don't Give Up'. I have another version by Willie Nelson and Sinead O'Connor. There is an ocean of difference between Gabriel, an ex-Genesis lead singer and explorer of African music, and Nelson, the grand old man of American country. But truths unite us all. The song starts:

> In this proud land we grew up strong
> We were wanted all along
> I was taught to fight, taught to win

> *I never thought I could fail ...*
> *No fight left or it seems*
> *I am a man whose dreams have all deserted ...*
> *No one wants you when you lose ...*

Man as god suddenly becomes man in crisis. The woman tries to comfort him:

> *Don't give up because you have friends ...*
> *Don't give up ... I know you can make it good ...*

But this man's life is going downhill; he does not have a job, then he loses his home:

> *Moved on to another town*
> *Tried hard to settle down*
> *For every job so many men*
> *So many men no one needs ...*

You can hear the dry emptiness in Willie Nelson's voice; the man can't take anymore. Sinead O'Connor is sweet, reasoning and sensual, as she uses everything she can to keep him functioning. Like a mantra, she repeats:

> *Don't give up ... 'cos you have friends*
> *Don't give up ... You're not the only one*
> *Don't give up ... No reason to be ashamed*
> *Don't give up ... You still have us*
> *Don't give up now ... We're proud of who you are*
> *Don't give up ... You know it's never been easy*
> *Don't give up ... 'cos I believe there's a place ... There's a place where we belong.*

Men in crisis need to be told, repeatedly: 'Don't give up. You have friends, you have family, you have people who love you and believe in you. Don't give up. There is a place for us.'

But many women are disappointed in their men; the qualities they loved are often only skin-deep.

'Inside, men are like pressure cookers.' JILL

The man will rarely see the woman's problem. And if she dares to complain, he snaps. She could say, 'Pull yourself together', but nothing will be accomplished. She must play her man using all her skills. As he strains away, give him more line. As he relaxes and tires, reel him in.

'Men are inflexible; women are adaptable.' SANDY

Defuse his violence and bit by bit, you defuse the violence in this land. We can double the police force, and we must teach our youth good values. Yet the fires are already burning and women can put them out. If sweet reason fails, then other tactics need to be employed. The female psychologist must become the female spy.

Women know where the guns are hidden, or at least they have a good idea. They know if their men are turning rotten inside. Some women encourage them, some give their admiration, while many look the other way. They know, but why should they tell? (And who can they trust to tell – other men?) Better a rotten man to look after them than no man at all. It's the ultimate male trick. Except it doesn't work as well as it once did.

The maid brigade

'This is the first Christmas in seven years that we're going away,' Teresa Griffiths told us as we were served tea on the patio of her Bryanston home. 'Before we were too nervous because we didn't want to come back to a ransacked house. From the beginning of December to the new year, you heard alarms every night. And no one got caught. It was a thieves' paradise, until Maggie and her friends came together.'

Maggie, who had been serving us tea, is Teresa's live-in domestic worker and nanny. She is a natural story-teller, and her eyes grow round as she begins: 'Last December an old, old granny was in the Bryanston shopping centre. I was with Miss Teresa; we had gone to buy dogfood. Miss Teresa was talking to a friend in the hairdresser's and I was by the car, thinking, 'shame this lady is so old', when a boy ran up and put a knife to her throat.

'He grabbed her purse and knocked her down on the pavement. Then he turned and walked away. I was so angry I ran after him shouting, "Stop the skollie!" Men looked at me like I was mad, but two friends saw me and we chased him to the road. He turned and waved his knife at us, but my friend kicked him in the leg and then I punched once-twice like I see Tshabalala do it on TV.' When Maggie redelivered her left hook for our benefit, followed by a crashing right cross, I saw how a suburban legend was born.

The skollie was knocked cold and taken into custody. The shopping mall held a party for Maggie and her friends. The old lady was there, too, in a wheelchair. She had broken her arm in the fall, but it was mending. Giving the toast to 'my three brave women' in the marquee, she said: 'We women did not start this nonsense, but you have shown we can stop it.'

That inspired Maggie and her friends to start The Maid Brigade of Mount Street, a professional blockwatch made up of female domestics. They roam the streets by day in pairs, with a cell phone and a sjambok hidden in the pockets of their uniforms. At night they cruise the area in an old green Toyota. They know who's who, the couples who are fighting and where the trouble often starts. Suspicious loiterers and unknown parked cars are reported to the police. Although The Maid Brigade is not armed, they have been given combat training, to the surprise and subsequent capture of two gangs who tried to rob local homes. Now the word has spread through the underworld: Don't mess with the Maid Brigade.

The women have formed a business co-operative that charges the residents of the block they live in and patrol. Most are happy to pay, especially now that they can dispense with the services of other private security firms.

'The others only come when there is already trouble,' Margaret said. 'We are here to make sure trouble never starts.'

Maid Brigades are forming across Gauteng, and women only can apply. If there were men, Maggie said, there would be two kinds of problems. Firstly, the men would try to take over, and secondly, the maids' husbands would be jealous.

'The old granny is right. We women never start the trouble but we can stop it. Any more tea?'

Community News, December 2004

the power of women

Women rarely create great symphonies or paintings. There have been world-class female authors but not many dramatists or poets. In 100 Poems by 100 Poets, an anthology compiled by Harold Pinter, only 11 of the selected 100 are female. Advertising is mostly aimed at women, but most of the award-winning creators are men. In recent UK Design and Art Direction awards, regarded by many as setting the world standard, almost 80 per cent of the winning copywriters and art directors were male. Is it that men are more creative? Or is it, as one novelist said, 'If I could create a child, I would never have the need to create a book'. Or is there a deeper reason?

Creativity is often a solo effort, or at the most, a team of two. Men are natural soloists, whilst women work most effectively in groups, from female co-operatives that arise in the poorest areas around the world to book clubs in the affluent suburbs. An ardent feminist told me that polygamy is not such a bad thing. It allows a community of women to be together in some comfort, with only occasional disturbances from the man. Women in a group find it far easier to talk about deep personal issues than a group of men. Guys need the pub, raucous jokes and yesterday's rugby match to get along. Women sip their tea and cut deep.

Of course, women can be outstanding individualists. Look at prime ministers such as Margaret Thatcher and Benazir Bhutto. But do they succeed at the expense of a part of themselves? From 'Thatcher, Thatcher, milk snatcher' when she was minister of education to her cabinet wets when she reigned, the iron lady lost touch with her compassion. Bhutto ruled a country awash with violence and tainted with the worst record of child exploitation in the world. Even Golda Meir was no loving earth mother. Success in a man's world has its price.

A woman's universe is one of mutual support. The power comes from the group. It is not always on the side of peace and love. During the First World War, it was the women's taunts and praise that drove men to the fronts filled with mud and corpses. In KwaZulu-Natal, women have whipped up their men into a brew of violence and revenge.

the women of africa

Women, as a group, will move this country either into prosperity or to war. Man is in shock, which could be toxic or not. Ladies, the choice is yours. You cannot leave the decision to the few in parliament and the corporate world. You are scorned, battered and abused. How much can you absorb until you lose your self-respect? Queen Latifah raps:

U N I T Y ...
U N I T Y ...
You gotta let them know ...
You ain't a bitch or a ho* ...

* 'Ho', short for 'whore', is African-American male ghetto-speak for a woman, as in, 'Come here, ho' or 'Buy me cigarettes, ho'.

And Annie Lennox sings to the sisters:

The sweetest woman in the world
can be the meanest woman in the world ...
It's a thin line between love and hate ...

If the thin line is crossed and a woman's hate is stronger than her love, the human race is in fatal trouble. There is still time for sisters to help the sisters, for the fortunate élite to reach out and embrace the struggling many, and for the sorority of support to spread across Africa and the world.

sex, money and ancient greece

Aristophanes wrote a play called *Lysistrata* about 2 500 years ago. The protagonist is a beautiful, high-class Athenian who is fed up with all the wars. Her husband and sons are taken away, doing pointless men's things. She brings a group of women together and, after some convincing, they agree to go on a sex strike. They will meet their husbands 'lightly clad in transparent gowns of Amorgos silk', but it is a case of 'don't touch until you agree to peace'. If the men threaten to force themselves on their wives, Lysistrata suggests they submit, but take and show no pleasure.

The men's view is that their wives are poking their noses where they don't belong. Women must weave, while men go to war. Lysistrata then makes the following declaration: 'The War shall be women's business'. Aristophanes is a bawdy Greek, and as the men grow hard, their warlike resolutions grow soft. Unable to stop what they had started, they rely on the victorious women to make the peace treaties.

No more war was the objective, and denial of sex was the tactic. The strategy, however, was financial control:

> Magistrate (addressing the women): I would ask you first, why ye have barred our gates?
>
> Lysistrata: To seize the treasury. No more money; no more war.
>
> Magistrate: Then money is the cause of the war?
>
> Lysistrata: And of all our troubles.

When the women of Athens bonded together, they were unstoppable. While sex as a weapon may be degrading and dangerous, the strategy of financial control is still valid. When the women of Africa become financially independent, they will help their men from a position of strength.

'Men can't all be exported, but puppies can be trained.' PRUE F

twenty-three
the squatter camp in the boardroom

10 x 2010

After the Amandla Statues are unveiled, three jets will fly over in close formation, laser-writing '10 x 2010' in the early evening sky. '10 x 2010' represents the national six-year plan to reach the top 10 in the World Competitiveness League by 2010. That will put South Africa ahead of most countries in Europe.

After the ceremonies, the party will begin. The Arch of Democracy is being turned into the world's largest music stage for an all-night Afro-Hop with mopane burgers and marula lite beer.

World Internet News, 27 April 2004

A significant part of Singapore's economic success is due to its '2020 vision' that simply says by 2020 the average Singaporean will earn as much as the average American. Political and civic organisations have bought into this vision and while citizens can debate tactics, they all agree on where they want to go. Visions are now being expressed by countries, corporations and cities to focus attention on the bigger picture and give purpose to a myriad of activities; but visioning is not a new fad.

'Where there is no vision, the people perish.' PROVERBS XXIX – 18

renaissance dawning

A vision helps us to see beyond the daily grind, encourages us to invest in our future and children, and shows us that a shared picture of tomorrow can heal the wounds of the past. Any shared vision is founded on awareness and acceptance of current issues. We cannot go forward unless we know where we currently are. And together with the vision we need shared values – if vision is the 'what' we want to achieve, values become the 'how'.

Then the vision is divided into objectives, strategies and plans, while the values are turned into policies. Creating dreams of the future is no idle exercise; it is a process that encourages commitment and focuses energy.

Whether we beneficiate gold, create mopane-burgers, make a trade alliance with India or re-ruralise southern Africa is all open to debate. I have thrown together a handful of provocations that are designed to stimulate thought. It is fashionable for the previously advantaged to dismiss all positive scenarios with statements like 'Africa is going to the dogs'. Sadly, they may be right, especially if enough join the doom-sayers. Self-fulfilling prophecies of failure, like a child saying he will fail his exams then proving he is right, are distressingly common. Instead let us affirm that South Africa can be a winning nation. Then the only question remaining is 'how?'.

The process starts with shared awareness.

how the other 80% live

It had been raining for a week, and Joseph the messenger had not been at work for three days. Everyone was irritable; deliveries piled up and secretaries had to brave the miserable weather to make sure the most urgent material reached its destination. When Joseph came back, everyone gave him a good telling off, especially when he started to explain that it was the rain.

Eventually the tea-lady told me.

The rain had washed away Joseph's shack, and inside it one of his twin baby daughters. He had been searching for her through the storms, the chaos, rivers of mud, floating furniture and drowned possessions. *The Star* had carried a small front-page story on the

the squatter camp in the boardroom

incident. I had read it and felt a momentary pain, but not for a moment did I connect our Joseph with the Joseph in the article.

Our Joseph was a quiet, small, thin man, looking older than his years. He was always willing to help, and so he ended up doing the messiest jobs. It became a case of: 'Just ask Joseph'. None of us knew where he lived or of his twin baby girls, until one was dead. And so after the tragedy, and our embarrassed expressions of sympathy, it was business as usual.

Ubuntu: you are what others perceive you to be. When we saw Joseph at all, it was as a cog in the machine. And how did he see us? I simply do not know.

But I do know that South Africa will never achieve anything like her true potential until her people are tied by bonds of understanding and respect, not shackled by the chains of ignorance and fear.

Yet we do remain ignorant of each other. Or, to be more accurate, whites remain ignorant of blacks. We impose our religion over time-honoured customs. We deride ancestral worship and then pray to 'our Father', the 'holy ghost' and preach of a man who can turn water into wine and rise from the dead. We impose on others our medicine made in distant laboratories while paying little regard to herbal remedies found in our fields and forests.

Many white South Africans have no black friends. White business-people will occasionally make a township field visit, under strict supervision, then regale dinner parties with tales of their great adventure. Few of the privileged classes have seen how the other 80% live. Very few have ever attended a rural wedding, a township street party or funeral. And has any white you know spent a night in a shack settlement?

I remember a UK advertising poster for Guinness that says 'I don't like it because I've never tried it' and many whites do not like blacks simply because they have not tried to get to know them. They are madams and masters to the gardener and maid (still often called 'the boy' and 'the girl') and think other blacks moving into the neighbourhood are lowering its tone.

The CEO of a major South African corporation told me that the majority of his staff are lazy, greedy and disruptive, 'members of the underclass'. He did not see the irony of his underclass speaking two to

209

six languages, while he could speak only one. It comes as no surprise that his corporation is strike-prone and underperforming.

Mother Theresa was asked why she insisted that the powerful and famous who visited her must also go to the poor and sick tended to by her order. She replied that awareness is all-important, because awareness leads to concern. Then concern leads to love, and love leads to service. Without awareness we will be quick to judge, slow to care and even slower to help.

Of course, visiting townships can be a relatively dangerous experience and not to be indulged in too often if you drive a new Mercedes. While everyone should quickly become more township aware, it will be a long time before the boardroom goes to the squatter camp. And so the squatter camp must enter the boardroom. Here are a few practical ways to start:

- *Read another newspaper*

Regularly reading The Sowetan has given me ongoing insights into our parallel universe. While Business Day will tell me about the economic impact of a strike, The Sowetan is more likely to discuss the strikers' grievances. Magazines like Bona, Drum, True Love and Pace introduce me to other heroes, struggles and dreams. Radio Metro opens my ears to music and language while a pot-pourri of TV programmes open my eyes.

- *Research what others think*

Jack Welch of GE says there are only two research measures he cares about: the levels of employee and customer satisfaction. Everything else flows from these. There are many research techniques and it is easy to drown in information. Concentrate on less data, more insight. And no formal research takes the place of you listening to the stories of other lives.

- *Support a farm school*

Or a refuge for abused women, or township basketball ... But don't let the support be only financial, become involved. Spend a half-day, two to four times a year, teaching at the farm school, and learning.

- *Take the township tour*

As sanitised as it is, you will still breathe in the spirit of the place. I have been with SAB reps on memorable tavern tours of Soweto, and with various marketing executives on field trips to urban and rural areas around the country. Each one has added to my store of knowledge.

stories of a new south africa

It is a time for us to have stories to share. The boardrooms and squatter camps need common ground. In the old South Africa, our stories were divisive, from the Voortrekker Monument to 'one settler, one bullet' spray-painted on walls.

The new South Africa began with a story the world saw and marvelled at; created by those patient, hopeful queues of voters on 27 April 1994. More stories were soon written; by the gaunt, dying Joe Slovo, an ex-commissar of red menace who drove the housing accord through in his last months. By President Mandela in his number six Springbok rugby shirt, and by Jonah Lomu in the World Cup final running with the ball eight times, and being stopped eight times by *Amabokoboko!*

The progress to the 1995 world championship is a modern morality tale: from the initial highlight of beating Australia to disgrace against Canada, the triumphant return of Chester Williams, redemption in the mud against France and, finally against the odds, the glory. Things are never easy for the children of Africa. We are capable of surprises and resilience, yet sometimes we do stupid things and act violently. When we decide to help each other, we can take on the world.

All the changes in South Africa and the world make this place and this time a turning point in history. We will be judged by our employment record, not by our millionaires, by the progress of our nation, not a few individuals; by the potential of our youth and by war or peace.

A nation is most of all judged by the people who succeed in it. South Africa has a prisoner turned president; Panama has a president turned prisoner. In the smoky gloom of an early winter's evening, a young black schoolgirl sits with her books in front of her family's makeshift shack, using the last thin rays of sunlight to study. When we build the legend of a better society (and it will take more than a generation), the world will beat a path to our door.

the african renaissance and world competitiveness

The African renaissance is a vision that needs specific goals and objectives. Otherwise it is too easy to claim victory – is another 100 jobs a renaissance – or too difficult – must we achieve American employment levels before we celebrate?

One measure that can be considered is world competitiveness. It is a measure that already exists, is comparative and covers most areas.

The World Competitiveness Project defines world competitiveness as 'the ability of a country or a company to, proportionally, generate more wealth than its competitors in world markets'. The report measures the inherited and created assets of a country, the processes that transform these assets into economic results and the degree of internationalisation that gives each country the ability to test its formula in global markets. The criteria range from growth and export diversification to education standards and society values.

As competitiveness increases wealth, it creates new assets for the benefit of the next generation, while a wealthy, uncompetitive country is spending its children's inheritance. South Africa consistently sits near the bottom of the competitiveness table. Out of over 40 countries measured, we hover around the middle to late 30s.

Being in the top 20 is a minimum requirement for the world to take us seriously. The top 10 defines a winning nation. It is a target that requires fast and fundamental change orchestrated at a national level. In 1994 many thought the country had re-invented itself and taken a short-cut to the economic high road. But the government has dithered, trying to satisfy the many factions of its alliance, whilst coming to terms with world economic realities. Bureaucracy, cumbersome at best, hopelessly corrupt at worst, gobbles up resources and produces little of value. And companies have stayed on a path of cautious, incremental change; being New South Africa-friendly is the price they pay to win a contract, not a deep-rooted belief in their destiny and that of this continent.

World competitiveness is a harsh discipline. Globally, there are far more people than jobs. South Africa has to develop and market its world competencies. We are not, nor will we ever be, cost leaders, but we must cut costs dramatically, simply to survive. In two industries, tourism and mining, we offer differentiation that can be leveraged. In other industries there are a wealth of opportunities on a local, regional and global scale, some of which have been explored in this book. But very few of these opportunities will be realised whilst we remain a nation divided. Whites are greedy and racist; blacks are lazy and violent, coloureds are drunks and Indians are crooks – there are truths in all stereotypes, and as long as we accentuate the negatives, we will discover the most self-destructive, self-fulfilling prophecies of all.

When South Africans share one vision and a common set of values, we will discover that more unites than separates us and instead of finding ways to pull each other down, we will find a way forward that synthesises the best of us. The word 'renaissance' means re-birth, implying that the paths to the future can be found by rediscovering the values of the past. An African renaissance will not happen by following in the footsteps of America, Europe and Japan. We need to find our own voices, our own harmonies.

'If we try to play like the Brazilians we will never beat Brazil. If we try to play like the Germans we can never beat Germany. But if we learn to play like South Africans, there is no limit to what we can do.' CLIVE BARKER, *former coach of 'Bafana Bafana'*

join the afristocracy

By 2010, some of the children first tempted to attend school by a Mandela sandwich will be graduating from universities and technikons. If things go well for this country, they will have a wonderful selection of career opportunities and a fine selection of local role-models, a new breed of Afristocrats who succeed through their abilities. The new Afristocracy will be articulate, compassionate, young and probably photogenic. Children will have a modern-day Valhalla filled with their own twenty-first century heroes. If things go well.

If things don't go well, this country will be edgy at best, or it could slide into chaos. When a wind blows your ship towards the rocks, it is natural to look at them. But when you do, you steer towards disaster. It is hard to tear your eyes away and look where you need to go to be safe. Do it and you steer that way. That is also the theory behind self-fulfilling prophecies and the reason this quest for blue skies began.

We have the capability. We are blessed with a wealth of natural assets. All we need, which is also the hardest thing for us to have given all the anger and hurt, is a positive and shared belief in our future. We need projects to unify us. And then the motivation to take the first step.

> 'If the world has not approached its end, it has reached a major watershed in history, equal in history to the turn from the Middle Ages to the Renaissance. It will demand from us a spiritual blaze . . .
>
> This ascension is similar to climbing onto the next anthropological stage. No one on earth has any other way left — but upward.' ALEXANDR SOLZHENITSYIN

references and acknowledgements

Introduction:
Hamel, G and Prahalad, CK, *Competing for the Future*, Harvard Business School Press, USA, 1994.

One: The Arch of Democracy
The World Competitiveness Report is published by the World Competitive Project.
Page 1: Angus Greig generously shared his triumphal arch and column with me.
Page 2: President Mandela, near the beginning of his autobiography, passes on the wisdom of how a shepherd leads; he was told the story in his youth. Mandela, NR, *Long Walk to Freedom*, MacDonald Purnell, South Africa, 1994.
Page 4: *The Art of War*, written 2000 years ago by Sun Tzu, a Chinese warrior-philosopher, has become an international guide for strategists, business and political leaders. Many of his Taoist contradictions, like 'to win without fighting is best', have been studied in Japan and their post-war economic ascendancy owes much to his teachings (my copy is a translation by Thomas Cleary, Shambala Publications, USA, 1991).
Page 5: Ubuntu has been proposed as a social, business, political and religious force. 'We are saying to corporations that there is such a

215

thing as being African – there are values such as compassion and sharing, and philosophies and an orientation to life which are traditionally African.' Reuel Khoza interviewed by *Enterprise*, October 1994. However 'the trouble is that ubuntu seems to mean almost anything one chooses.' *The Economist*, March, 1995.

Page 9: Information on the South African Homeless People's Federation comes from the People's Dialogue on Land Shelter.

Two: Welcome to the USSA

Thanks to Dr Richard Cornwell and Jurie Snyman for their enlightening crash courses in southern Africa's realities and potential.

Page 14: The Kenya, Zimbabwe and South Africa economic alliance is discussed by Professor Peter Nanyenya Takirambudde in *Africa Insight*, No. 3, 1993.

Page 14: The Mozambican option has been explored by political strategists in the landlocked countries.

Page 15: Afro-cops: see 'Neighbourhood watch in Southern Africa', *The Economist*, 3 December 1994.

Page 16: Intermediate Technologies: see 'Turning Dreams into Reality' by Bronwen Jones, *Enterprise*, February 1995.

Three: The ocean that joins us

Thanks to Rajiv Shrivastava from the Consulate General of India for his help and contacts. Statistics from a variety of published sources including the *CIA World Factbook*, 1998.

Page 24: *More Affordable Housing*: the aims and achievements of Hudco are expressed in their various publications.

Page 25: *Opportunities for Trade between India and South Africa* is published by the commercial section of the Consulate General of India; India Online publishes current opportunities on the Internet.

Four: Three-wheeling through Africa

Thanks to DA Crook of Making Africa Mobile for an update on three-wheelers and to Stuart Blinder for his story of the three-wheeler ice-cream millionaire.

Page 33: The Hot Box has been designed by Meinrad Bodner.

Five: Can you make money out of the poor?
Thanks to Dr Ettienne van Loggerenberg and Victor Nosi for their time, knowledge and insights. Thanks to Clem Sunter for providing the spark.

Page 36: The banking table with three queues exists in Indonesia.

Page 38: 'The things we want most from a bank' (township research):
1. to be here
2. small business loans
3. to do something for the pensioners
4. home loans.

Page 39: Information on Grameen Bank from *Scientific American*, *American Banker* and the *Internet*.

Page 42: *Fortune*, 4 April, 1994. Since 1991, companies have spent more on computers and communications equipment than on industrial, mining, construction and farm machines.

Six: What can you do with dirt?
Thanks to Alan Stokes, Andile Ncontsa and Piers Kenyon who have spent many patient hours opening my eyes; to Victor Khanye and members of the Development Association who welcomed me to their meetings. Victor died in a car crash in 1998. It is a tragic loss for his family, many friends and the community of Boteng that he so magnificently served. Thanks also to Dr Norman Reynolds of The Market Association who explained the economic theory and practical needs of markets in southern Africa; and to the 'Dukester' for the title.

Page 48: For a colourful description of the night markets of Benin see the article 'Between the Lines: African Civil Society and the Remaking of Urban Communities' by Dr Abdou Maliqalim Simone in *Africa Insight*, No. 3, 1992.

Seven: Better than money
Background information from the Internet and a variety of magazine articles including 'The Billion Dollar Swop Shop' by Nigel Healey in *Management Today*, April 1994.

Page 54: Ithaca Hours is explained in 'The Ultimate Barter' by Michelle Silver, *Mother Earth News*, August/September 1993.

Eight: Back to the land
Background information from Policies for a new urban future, published by the Urban Foundation, 1990.
Page 62: 'Comparative lessons for land reform in South Africa' by Professor Fanie Cloete, Africa Insight, No. 4, 1992.

Nine: De-engineering: The cure for Sandtonitis
Page 65: 'Marketing myopia' by Theodore Levitt, Harvard Business Review, 1975.
Page 70: Thanks to James Porter for introducing me to the biggest Spar in the world.
Page 71: Focus and sacrifice are amongst The 22 Immutable Laws of Marketing by Al Ries and Jack Trout, HarperBusiness, USA.
Page 72: 'Marketing Myopia' by Theodore Levitt.
Page 74: Own-label has reached another level with President's Choice in Loblaws, Canada. As they cannot sell beer in their own outlets, Loblaws President's Choice beer is now being sold in independent bottle stores. Own-label has crossed the threshold. Thanks to Wendy and Nick Boothman for a Canadian perspective (and good times).

Ten: The bigger picture
Thanks to Carol Grolman, Ivan Weltman, Joe Lukhele, Mike Rossi, Peter Vundla, Robyn Putter, Sam Michel and Sonwabile Ndamase for their conversations and inspiration.
'Gamekeepers' is based on COMPRA, a security company started by two highly impressive ex-prisoners in the Johannesburg CBD.
Page 76: 'The globalisation of markets', Theodore Levitt, Harvard Business Review, 1983, elaborates on the wisdom of one washing machine versus many. His thinking influenced the Saatchi brothers who created a global agency network that began in Golden Square, Soho.
Page 76: 'The Fortune Global 500', Fortune, 1998.

Eleven: Never rub bottoms with a porcupine
Thanks to Sarah da Vanzo for a treasure trove of ideas and information.
Page 89: The display of Akan gold is one of the most interesting exhibits I have found on the Internet. (http://www.fa.indiana.edu/conner/africart/home.html)

references and acknowledgements

Thanks to Dr Martha Ehrlich and Dr Michael Connor.

Twelve: Hooked on hemp
Thanks to James Wynn and Tessa Sonik for their insights on the commercial potential of hemp. Thanks to Robert Sherwood for his research and the House of Hemp for their literature.

Page 102: Everett Koop, a recent surgeon general in the United States, accepted the use of dagga for a number of medical conditions, including cancer, glaucoma and multiple sclerosis.

Page 102: 'The case for (and against) cannabis', *Face* magazine, October 1993, and Internet contributions to the new South African constitution regarding dagga, provided background information.

Thirteen: Return of the wrigglies
Page 108: Figures extracted from Grolier's *American Academic Encyclopedia* and reference works on the Internet.

Page 109: References for edible bugs: *Scientific American*, August 1992; *Mother Earth News*, June 1993; *Science World*, October 1993; *Sierra*, November 1994; *Esquire*, March 1995 (merci, Genres) *You*, 6 April 1995; *Fuma food from Africa*, Renate Coetzee, Butterworths, South Africa, 1982.

Page 111: The commercial possibilities and ecological benefits of the prolific earthworm can be found on the Internet home pages of Green Hut.

Page 112: Thanks to Ben Ditshego for giving me my first taste of mopane worms (fried, chewy and nuttyish).

Page 114: Recipes courtesy of Brenda Halstead.

For more information see the *Food Insects Newsletter*, published by the University of Wisconsin.

Fourteen: Adventures in cyberspace
Thanks to all my digital connections who have taken the time to educate this technopeasant. Ongoing information from *Newsweek*, *Wired*, *Mail & Guardian* and the Internet itself.

Page 125: Cyberporn is a heated issue. 'On a Screen Near You: Cyberporn' by Philip Elmer-DeWitt, in the 3 July (year?) issue of *Time* was later discredited, and Internet defenders claim that there is more science than pornography in cyberspace. The reality is that anyone with a computer, a modem and an enquiring nature can spend 24 hours a day, every day, engrossed in porn and perversion.

Page ?: The Virtual University is available in South Africa through Videre, a Dimension Data company.

Fifteen: Siyabonga

Page 129: Australian figures from Australian Tourism on the Internet.

Page 129: South African tourism figures from Satour.

Page 130: These three strategic options, based on writings by Michael Porter and Philip Kotler, are the basis of strategic software programs like Business Insight, produced by Business Resource Software.

Sixteen: The Joburg jol

Thanks to all who partook in the Johannesburg visioning process, for sharing their ideas about the rebirth of a great African city. Thanks to Thami Nxasana, my co-facilitator in the process, who showed me a familiar world through different eyes.

Page 141: Statistics taken from *Policies for a new urban future* published by The Urban Foundation, 1990.

Page 146: Newtown history extracted from 'Newtown: The People and the Place' by Arlene Segal and Elsabe Brink in *Planning and History Study Group Symposium: Places, People and Planning,* vol. 1, 1994.

Seventeen: It's better that Bournemouth

Page 155: Thanks to Elsa Evans, manager of San Sereno, Sister Steffie and all the nurses at Frail Care.

Nineteen: Flowers of the east

Background information from Ash Resources and Hudco.

Page 165: 'India eye constructive use of fly ash', *Coal and Synfuels Technology,* 9 May 1994.

Page 166: 'Indian firms build with fly ash' *Coal and Synfuels Technology,* 16 January 1995.

Page 166: Biofly was developed in the engineering department of Woolongong University.

references and acknowledgements

Page 167: In Canada there are 50-year-old wooden bridges that withstand temperatures that range from -35 to 100 degrees Fahrenheit, humidity, snowstorms, the odd tornado and Mack Trucks.

Page 167: N-Viro soil was featured in Environmental Decisions, December 1990.

Page 167: The horticulturist is Simon Wilson.

Page 168: A chrysanthemum stem, including packaging, weighs approximately 100 grams. Five million stems a week is equivalent to 500 tons of cargo. The best quality stems would be for export; the rest could be sold locally (and brighten up the side of the road). But what would the jumbo jets bring back to make the round trip worthwhile?

Page 169: 'Fly ash tested as a haven for oysters', Coal and Synfuels Technology, 25 July 1994.

Page 169: 'Fly ash brings in bucks for plant operator', Coal and Synfuels Technology, 16 January 1995.

Page 169: Eskom Annual Environmental Report, 1998.

Page 171: Of Love and Barley, Basho, translated by Lucien Stryk, Penguin, Great Britain, 1985.

Twenty: The Third World War

Thanks to Dr Ruben Sher for his assessment of Africa's battle against AIDS.

Page 173: HIV and AIDS projections: Peter R Doyle, The impact of AIDS on the South African population.

Twenty-one: *Educere:* To draw out

Page 183: Thanks to Rev Grant Evans and the dedicated teachers for their time. Thanks also to the headmaster and 175 children of the farm school one hour's drive from Sandton City that is without water, electricity or a telephone.

Page 187: Statistics on the lack of scientists: JB Clark, 'The intraregional transfer of technology', Africa Insight, No. 1, 1991.

Page 190: Background information and statistics from the White Paper on Sport.

Page 190: Population statistics: JL Sadie, *A Projection of the South African Population 1991-2011*, Bureau of Market Research, UNISA, 1993.
Page 191: Thanks to Steve Harris for the music information.
Page 192: Thanks to Madala Mphahlele for his time and wisdom.

Twenty-two: The women of Africa

Thanks to Madeline Lass, who gave me a wide-ranging introduction to feminism.
Page 195: *The Rainbow*, DH Lawrence, William Heinemann Ltd, Great Britain, 1915.
Page 196: The Tanzanian experience is related in: *African Women: Our Burdens and Struggles*, Ruth Besha (ed.), The Institute for African Alternatives, Johannesburg, 1994.
Page 197: The problem with men: much of the analysis is based on 'Masculinity in Crisis?', Jenny Lemon, *Agenda*, No. 24, 1995.
Page 199: They should all be exported: During a group discussion on feminism, a respondent remembers hearing Jenny Crwys-Williams expressing this sentiment on Radio 702.
Page 200: 'Don't Give Up', Peter Gabriel, EMI Music (SA).
U N I T Y, Dana Owens and Joe Sample, Motown.
'Thin line between love and hate', R Poindexter, R Poindexter and J Members, Tusk.

Liz Mitchell, librarian at the Johannesburg Chamber of Commerce and Industry, tracked down many of my obscure requests. Musiwalwo Philemon Dzhuihuho tracked down many others. To all of you ... *siyabonga*.